NINJITSU
FOR
WOMEN

Ninja Secrets of
Defensive Fighting

ASHIDA KIM

k

CITADEL PRESS
Kensington Publishing Corp.
www.kensingtonbooks.com

CITADEL PRESS books are published by

Kensington Publishing Corp.
850 Third Avenue
New York, NY 10022

All Kensington titles, imprints, and distributed lines are available at
special quantity discounts for bulk purchases for sales promotions,
premiums, fund raising, educational, or institutional use. Special book
excerpts or customized printings can also be created to fit specific needs.
For details, write or phone the office of the Kensington special sales man-
ager: Kensington Publishing Corp., 850 Third Avenue, New York, NY
10022, attn: Special Sales Department, phone 1-800-221-2647.

Kensington and the K logo Reg. U.S. Pat. & TM Office
Citadel Press is a trademark of Kensington Publishing Corp.

First printing 2000

10 9 8 7 6 5 4 3 2 1

Library of Congress Cataloging-in-Publication Data

Kim, Ashida.
    Ninjitsu for women : ninja secrets of defensive fighting
    / Ashida Kim.
        p. cm.
    "A Citadel Press book."
    ISBN 0–8065–2145–7 (pb)
    1. Ninjutsu. 2. Self-defense for women.   I. Title.
    GV1114.73.K564   1999
    796.815—dc21   99–16393
                                                                CIP

NINJITSU
FOR
WOMEN

Also by Ashida Kim

The Invisible Ninja
Iron Body Ninja
Ninja Mind Control
Secrets of the Ninja

Contents

Preface

It is said that *ninjitsu* is a "dark art," mysterious, sinister, and therefore yin—the yielding, feminine, inner life of things—making it well-suited for study and use by women warriors. We present here, for the first time, a glimpse at how the hidden sisterhood of feudal Japan can be of use to any woman. Presented herein are the methods whereby women can overcome more powerful adversaries. These techniques of combat are based on instinct and directed at attacking vulnerable and vital areas of the body, thus killing or crippling an enemy.

Revealed here are the forbidden fighting techniques and training methods of the Black Dragon kunoichi as handed down for the last seven hundred years. These martial arts skills are not for the squeamish or the weak at heart. They are part of the most effective, deadly, and vicious combat system ever devised—ninjitsu.

There are a good many books on self-defense, but here are the means to become a warrior. The Secrets of the Empty Hand enable anyone, regardless of size, speed, or skill, to kill, cripple, or maim any attacker. But ninjitsu is more than that. It is a martial art in which to train and study, explore and practice. The kunoichi of old were constantly surrounded by danger, yet through meditation, they not only survived but actually flourished. Far from living in constant fear, they learned to enjoy their lives.

One of the ways in which this is accomplished, even today, is the practice of *kumi-uchi*, or methods of unarmed combat. This teaches the agent balance and a sense of self-worth through accomplishment. The mastery of each technique adds to the confidence of the student, and the fighting spirit is concurrently developed through mind control.

It is my hope that this book can provide a means whereby the meek can live in peace, killing or harming only when threatened with death—for all life is precious and cannot be replaced.

This book is not only about self-defense, but also about self-empowerment. You need not be a helpless victim, even against physical abuse or intimidation.

Ninjitsu for Women will show you many methods of striking, hitting, pinching, and inflicting pain to effect escape. What you need is will and sufficient ruthlessness to be most effective—without guilt for having acted, or regret for having caused pain to someone who deserved it.

Among martial artists, and ninja, there are only three times when the use of force is permitted: to establish order; to maintain order; and to restore order. How does one know when things are out of order? When an attacker throws the first punch. Then the gloves are off.

While it is true that you may lose, it is certain that you will never win if you don't play. As Bruce Lee said, "Better to die a broken piece of jade than to live a life of clay."

Introduction: The *Kunoichi* (Dragon Lady)

The *kunoichi* (pronounced koo-noh-*ee*-chee), or "Dragon Lady," is far more than a mere female counterpart of the ninja—"Brother of the Night." She is a power unto herself. She represents silence, mystery, duality, and hidden influences at work. She is intensely perceptive, a keen and accurate observer capable of interpreting the most subtle nuances of thoughts or deeds. In action she is confident; in spirit, she is just and gracious to her enemies. Her movements are graceful and her balance exceptional. She is adaptable and able to use her talents to her best advantage. She possesses a calm dignity and persistent energy in all her affairs.

Derived from the same ethical and philosophical roots as the ninja, the kunoichi are quiet, hardworking, sensible, practical, and unassuming. They are ambitious in useful directions and rely on instinct and intuition rather than prescribed patterns of thought and movement. The Dragon Lady, like the spider, weaves her web of intrigue not only professionally but in almost every aspect of her daily life.

During the time of the tong wars, with the proliferation of secret societies, the splintering of traditional clans, and "sword hunts" against the ninja in Japan, many *ronin*, or masterless samurai, were spawned from the ranks of the original Five Families of the Silent Way. Some of these were the sole survivors of their clan. Some were the deposed princes of underground empires. Others were widows and orphans.

As these refugees drifted into the shadowy world of the *yakuza* (gangsters or gamblers) or become nomadic, searching for a leader or cause, it became apparent that many more women than men had survived these attempted exterminations by the warlords. This was due in large part to the man's natural instinct to protect women and children, to the point of sacrificing oneself to insure the survival of the line. Furthermore, it was often easier for a woman, even with children, to fade into the landscape and disappear, since women appear to pose less of a threat than their male counterparts. But this is a mistaken assumption.

On the mainland, the daughters of the Mandarins frequently survived their fathers' assassination by rival gangs. Sometimes they were even offered the dubious honor of wedding the new master of the house. Bear in mind that during this period, many women, especially of noble birth (or quasi-noble birth as in the case of the underworld), were raised with their feet bound, that is, tightly wrapped in bandages shortly after birth to keep them from growing. In this way, the woman would always require assistance to walk and would, of necessity, be in constant need of servants. Thus they were kept subservient to men. Inevitably, however, there came a time when one of the surviving females was sufficiently filled with the desire for revenge, and she decided to retaliate.

The daughter of one assassinated lord invited all the friends of her new husband to the wedding feast and promptly poisoned them. So there she was, with a full-scale drug operation in place, many retainers loyal to her family name, and a sudden reputation for ruthless efficiency. No wonder, then, that she became the new head of the clan, as unorthodox as that may have been for the day and age. Like many details of history, her real name is lost to time, but from that day onward she was known as the Dragon Lady. And that is the name given to women agents of the Black Dragon Fighting Society.

This is not to say that the women formed an auxiliary or support group. Rather, the sisterhood formed an alliance with their "brothers," yoking their talents to champion their causes. The concept of the equality of women is not new to the ninja, who have long recognized that the special talents of the female agent enable her to accomplish her mission in subtle ways. The training of the women is rigorous and thorough, as they are taught to use their abilities to accomplish their ends without fail.

Networks of the ninja often included female spies known as kunoichi. These medieval "Dianas of the Darkness" were sometimes trained in the arts of the geisha so they could use their femininity to learn vital secrets about enemy movements and intentions. In general, there are five types of female agents in the Japanese kunoichi system of designation. They are:

Chia Nu or "Daughter of the House." This woman would be trained for espionage. She would advance in rank and status as her level of experience increased.

Chia Mu or "House Mother." More of a technique than a real class of agent, this is a method whereby one kunoichi recruits other girls to work for her in gathering intelligence. The new girls are usually diverted from the covert goal of the mission and are directed against a common foe, who may or may not be the actual target.

Chen T'ou Nu or "Pillow Girl." This is similar to the above type, except that each peripheral agent is unaware of the others. Only the *fujen* (controller) receives information from all the field agents and knows the complete picture.

Kung Chu or "Tool." This is a kunoichi version of the "expendable" agent, usually hired for one mission or because of a particular skill or talent. They are normally well paid, but are not privy to the inner sanctums of the organization.

Yu Jen or "Fool." This may be a dupe, acting out of misguided loyalty, misdirected duty, or misinformation; or she may be an individual who is "forced to cooperate" by extortion or promises of bribes. She seldom realizes she is an agent for the enemy.

The kunoichi are masters of the art of *hsi-men jitsu* (*saiminjitsu*) in Japanese), the way of the Mind Gate, and are adept at manipulating the Five Feelings to achieve their goals. Kunoichi often play on an enemy's weakness, either by physical inducements or subtle psychological means guided by their intuition. While other cultures relegated their feminine members to secondary roles during wartime, the ninja not only put women in the field as agents and assassins, they employed their reasoning abilities to evaluate incoming intelligence and construct scenarios of future events. Naturally, such agents were highly motivated and schooled not only in the effective use of their mental faculties, but also in the control of their emotions.

These special agents, selected for their great beauty and trustworthiness, might find some way to catch the eye of an intended target either by subtly "dropping a scarf" or more boldly by presenting a skill as a performer or entertainer. Once in his good graces, the kunoichi could "interrogate" her victim by flattering him or taking an interest in his hopes and fears. Later, if it suited her plans, she could let him seduce her. This might be necessary to penetrate the enemy fortress or get the target alone. Once the victim had enjoyed the intimate pleasures of the kunoichi, for they were trained in the art of loving (called "flowery combat" in Japan) as well as the dark art of death, he was successfully lulled into a false sense of security.

There were many weapons available to the skillful agent, but the women were most notable for assassinating their targets with the long hair needles commonly used in the feudal period. This was a logical weapon for a women, and one almost certain to be on hand when needed. The weapon might be employed to penetrate the enemy heart (ice-pick fashion), throat (under the ear), or temple (the thin bones are easily broken). Her mission accomplished, the kunoichi would shed her disguise and be "swallowed up by the night." If needed, a second agent might be dispatched to aid in the escape.

Danger was a constant companion to a kunoichi. If she was discovered or captured, rape, torture, and lingering death were the rewards for her espionage career. Through careful and extensive training, the ninja are taught certain mental disciplines that enable them not only to endure and survive capture, but also to turn it to their advantage. Psychic and intuitive training teach the agent incredible physical control of the body. In the Hindu mystic, this might take the form of being "buried alive" in suspended animation for an extended period of time. For the kunoichi, the techniques included conscious relaxation of the pelvic area to prevent injury should they be raped. This required a state of mental calm which came only with practice.

Due to the physical violence and certain execution that the female spy would receive if she were apprehended, the kunoichi had to be a master of the psychological ploy. When accused, she would instantly analyze the reason for the accusation. If it could not be discredited, she would quickly determine the goal of the interrogator and to what lengths he would go to achieve it. In most cases, such a scenario included the male chief of security who had been compromised by this infiltration. He could usually be counted on to extract his own particular revenge since he had been outwitted by a "mere" woman. In the face of such a threat, the kunoichi were taught to show no fear and never to beg for mercy, since any display of weakness merely stimulated hostility and aggression.

Remembering the injunction to escape as quickly as possible, since every minute that passed decreased the chances of success, the kunoichi might make sexual overtures to the guard who escorted her to her cell or interrogation room. Once in a secluded spot, she might even help him to disrobe, at which time he would be vulnerable to attack or embarrassment. The modern agent would do likewise, but the lady interested in self-defense would take the opposite tack, that is, she would lure the attacker to a public area where there would be some chance of assistance from passersby.

There are, of course, some situations in which resistance is futile. At those times, surrender is not dishonorable. But if this course is chosen, the agent should not complain, cry, beg, squirm, fight, or threaten retaliation. If there is to be retaliation, she will have to survive, continue to gather intelligence, analyze the enemy, and observe his habits and distinguishing characteristics. If she is on a job, she will have to have cased the layout and be familiar with the best escape routes. And she should seize any opportunity to get away.

If the kunoichi chooses to fight, she will do so with all her being. The kunoichi are trained in much the same manner as their male counterparts and are equipped with an arsenal of deadly and debilitating strikes, such as the thumb gouge, the double-ear slap, and the knee-to-groin movement. In addition to the techniques of psychological warfare that form a large part of this feminine art, the variety of surprise attacks and "sucker punches" employed by these sisters of the night make them formidable indeed.

NINJITSU
FOR
WOMEN

1

THE DRAGON LADY FIGHTING SYSTEM

The ninja have always been believers in the dichotomy of the universe. For every positive there must be a counterbalancing negative. Good is recognized as good only because there is evil. And for each yang there must be an equal yin. So it is not unusual that they would train women as well as men in the deadly and devastating Art of Invisibility.

While it may be hard for a man to philosophically accept killing a fellow man, it is even more difficult for a woman, who must not only accept the idea rationally but also come to grips with it on a deeper, more intuitive level. Abhorrence of violence first observed in female agents eventually fades into cool professionalism. This stage of altered awareness leads to the inevitable conclusion: an agent who is capable in the field, an asset to any operation, and one with Nature.

It should be pointed out that there are no extraordinary men or women, only ordinary people who find themselves in extraordinary situations. Most of these situations, such as mortal combat, daring rescues, and amazing escapes, can be easily avoided in contemporary society. But, from time to time, an opportunity for a great adventure presents itself. At such a moment, one must choose whether to live or die; it would be wise to be ready for either.

It is said that the mood of the warrior is that of waiting; he waits for the enemy to appear. Any veteran will tell you that an army is either fighting or getting ready to fight. Such training and study may take a lifetime. So it is with the ninja, and especially the kunoichi, for within each of us lies the "sleeping dragon of violence," and woe be unto those who incur the wrath of the Ninja Dragon Lady.

Before one can begin the study of any martial art, one must prepare the body and the mind. It is my belief that each person should develop or already have a system of exercises that serves to tone the muscles, develop the balance and reflexes, and generally keep one in shape. Here is a basic form of meditative exercise to relax the mind and ready the student for the Great Work.

SANCHIN MEDITATION

From a standing position, feet together, bend the knees and lower the body to the mat. Once in the kneeling position, lay the instep down onto the mat and sit comfortably on your heels as in Figure 1. Keep your back straight, head up, eyes open and alert. Sit proudly. You are Karateka Kunoichi, Dragon Lady of the Ninja.

Focus your attention on the site of the "third eye" (center of the forehead) and relax. Place both palms down on the thighs and keep your shoulders level. Breathe slowly and deeply. Listen. If you are in class, this pose would be the one assumed at the command, "Ready, kneel," and would be used during the lecture part of the instruction. If you practice alone, listen for the sound of your own heartbeat. This will reassure you and remind you that you are alive. Then, when you are afraid and need power, you will hear your heartbeat and remember your training. This is due to the adrenaline pump that is triggered with the

FIGURE 1

FIGURE 2

FIGURE 3

psychological "fight or flight" instinct, when the adrenal glands ready the body for combat. By keying ninjitsu to the adrenal reaction in this way, fear becomes an ally instead of an enemy.

The foundation of any fighting system is its stance, or fighting position. There are numerous such poses, but only a few are especially suited to the Dragon Lady techniques. When selecting which of these is best suited to the individual, considerations should be comfort, balance, and ease of movement (grace).

Cat Stance

Figure 2 illustrates the cat stance of the kunoichi. Ninety percent of your weight is on your rear leg, 10 percent is on the lead leg with its bent knee and poised snap kick. Both thumbs are in line and held defensively at solar plexus level. The cat stance is excellent for a small, quick fighter who likes to employ darting movements directly along the line of engagement. The shoulders are rounded forward and the chin is down, tucking the jaw protectively inside the bones of the shoulder girdle. Both elbows are pressed against the ribs, allowing the upper arms to shield the torso. As should be apparent, balance is precarious and strong ankles are recommended.

Vanishing Stance

The vanishing stance, with arms folded defensively across the chest, is fundamental to any study of ninjitsu. From this pose (Figure 3) both hands are snapped forward to strike the enemy with a reverse tiger claw strike, or double ear slap. Sixty percent of the Dragon Lady's weight is on the back leg, 40 percent is on the lead leg. The shoulders are square to the enemy. The head is tucked defensively within the shoulder girdle. The leading knee is turned slightly inward to guard the groin. The feet are at right angles. The hips are lowered, and the *hara*, or center, is thus prepared for battle.

The Dragon Lady may take one of the two basic attitudes. She may firmly "fix the enemy's eye" to intimidate him, or avert her eyes and appear timid and then attack with a powerful *kiai* (spirit shout) and fix her eyes on the intended target for concentration and *kime* (focus).

Back-Leaning Stance

The back-leaning stance (Figure 4) is an excellent form to practice from. Seventy percent of the weight is on the rear leg, 30 percent on the lead. Both thumbs are aligned in front of the solar plexus, and the elbows are pressed against the sides. Again, the shoulders and hips are square and the feet are at right angles. This stance is best employed when "falling back" before the

FIGURE 4

enemy's attack, and then counterattacking strongly. It allows very good movement side to side, which makes it possible to evade the enemy's initial gesture. This would be used if the Dragon Lady wanted to let the enemy know she was ready to fight. Such a posture would encourage him to become cagey and approach with more caution. That alone may cause him to reconsider further action; at the least, it will blunt his attack by breaking its momentum.

Stance of Readiness

A variation of the classic closed fist stance, the stance of readiness implies that you will fight. The body is dynamically tensed and the power is then concentrated in the center and on the "iron

FIGURE 5

fists." The intent is for the agent to survive the enemy's initial attack and strike from deep within his sphere. This stance (Figure 5) might be used if one were trapped. Sixty percent of the weight is on the leading leg, 40 percent on the back. The arms may be crossed as shown to form a protective shield, or the elbows may be held against the sides and the Dragon Lady may "peek" over her fists. Any kick from this position would have to be performed with the rear leg, making it more powerful but also more likely to be seen and deflected.

Forward-Leaning Stance

The forward-leaning stance is found in almost all martial arts. As shown (Figure 6), 70 percent of the Dragon Lady's weight is

FIGURE 6

over the leading leg with its deeply flexed knee. The lead hand is held defensively in *gedan-barai* (low block) position, while the right hand is "loaded"—preparing for an intended strike—near the right ear.

Practice shifting forward from the stance of readiness into the forward-leaning stance, then "fade back" into the back-leaning stance and slip into the vanishing stance. From there, begin the sequence again. This practice will make you aware of subtle shifts in balance and range, which will enable you to capitalize on any opening in the enemy's defense.

BASIC KICKS

Forward Roundhouse Kick

Depress the enemy's hand with your leading hand and pull him down across the line of engagement to bend him forward from the waist (Figure 7). The Dragon Lady's stance is square to the enemy, and she directs her weight forward, making him "carry" this extra burden, which prevents him from stepping forward with his attack.

Pivot on the ball of the leading foot and turn in to the enemy with the rear leg bent at the knee. As he is bent over, snap out with your rear leg in a strong forward roundhouse kick to the back of his neck (Figure 8). This strike will normally daze or stun him. Other targets include the kidney, which could knock him out if struck directly on the adrenal glands, or the lead knee.

From this position, the kunoichi can step over the enemy's arm. Seize his wrist with both hands and sit on his shoulder. This is a crippling technique that severely dislocates the joint.

Back Kick

If the Dragon Lady is seized from behind by both wrists, the pain that this hold can inflict on both shoulders is severe. The enemy will try to keep both elbows locked to gain as much leverage as possible (Figure 9). The first tactic for escape is to try to turn at least one arm so that the elbow can be bent to relieve the pressure. Also, by stepping forward the kunoichi can put some distance between herself and the enemy. This small step can provide some measure of control over the potential force that can be directed against her back.

Although the enemy's position is fixed and known, the well-trained martial artist never uses a "blind" technique; she always looks over one shoulder or the other to pick a target. Lift the trailing leg and bend the knee. Bend slightly forward to improve

FIGURE 7

FIGURE 8

FIGURE 9

FIGURE 10

the angle of the strike and drive the heel of your foot straight back into the enemy's chest (Figure 10). Strike the solar plexus at the xiphoid process, a tiny chip of bone at the end of the sternum. This attack can tear the triangular bone free of its cartilage and drive it into the diaphragm. This renders the enemy breathless and causes hemorrhage and damage to the peritoneal and chest cavities.

Roundhouse Kick

The best offensive weapon for the Dragon Lady is her leg. The kunoichi seldom kicks above solar plexus level, since standing on one foot reduces balance. Today's muggers are aware of kicking techniques, so they must be dynamic and effective.

Mawashi-geri, the roundhouse kick, is one of the most powerful techniques available. In a forward-leaning stance, catch the enemy's arm and use it for balance and to pull him into the kick for added impact. Pivot on the ball of the left foot and load the right leg by bending it at the knee. Pull the enemy off balance as you turn in to him (Figure 11).

With a snapping action, strike out strongly to the enemy's torso. Attack with the shin, intending to knock the wind out of the enemy (Figure 12).

The shin kick is well-known in *muay thai* (Thai kickboxing), where the boxers kick trees with full force to train for the ring. Likewise, it is one of the easiest and most natural kicks in which the full body weight can be used in the strike.

Rear Heel Kick

The rear heel kick is a short snapping action directed against the enemy's shin, should he be so fortunate as to gain a rear arm choke. It is performed in three steps: lift the knee vertically, bending the leg 90 degrees; holding this angle, jerk the foot straight back against the enemy's knee (Figure 13); throw the enemy to the ground and finish him. With this strike, the inten-

FIGURE 11

FIGURE 12

FIGURE 13

FIGURE 14

tion is to break the knee. This requires forty pounds of pressure if the force is perpendicular to the kneecap, and twenty pounds if directed against the sides of the joint.

Furthermore, the heel can be driven down the shin in a painful scraping action, crushing the instep to prevent pursuit. Or, the back of the heel can be jerked up into the enemy's groin. However, remember the time lag here, and don't try this if he has a knife at your throat.

Side Kick

The side kick is one of the most basic kicks in the martial arts; it is also one of the most difficult to master. The striking surface may be the edge of the foot or the heel, and while the round-house kick may whip around to hit the enemy, the side kick lashes out along a linear path (Figure 14). To the skilled fighter, it is analogous to a lead jab. Since the legs are the longest weapons of the body, a snappy side kick can often be used to keep an enemy at bay.

Likely targets are the shin, knee, ankle, groin, lower abdomen, stomach, and solar plexus. The rear, or platform, leg must support the body, and the knee is flexed somewhat to facilitate this.

As with all kicking techniques: practice, perfect, then apply.

NINJITSU SELF-DEFENSE

The following are key to ninjitsu defense. Once they are ingrained into your response, you will experience your invincibility in both verbal and physical confrontations.

Security The ninja eliminates danger in several ways: by being aware of it; by not taking credit, so others do not become jealous; by not talking, to prevent gossip; and by not fighting, to bring peace and harmony.

Determination When confronted with the pillars of violence, the ninja knows, through resoluteness, the need to determine the outcome of the aggression, and he acts accordingly.

Calmness   The ninja's mind remains calm and composed in the face of violence. This permits calculation.

Conservation   To maintain optimum agility and endurance, the ninja avoids movements that are unnecessary or might be interpreted as aggressive.

Power   The goal of the ninja is to disrupt the balance of the enemy while retaining her own balance. In this way the enemy can be halted and control achieved.

Directness   The ninja accomplishes this by keeping the arms and legs as near as possible to the central balance of the body.

Pain   In training as well as in the application of the techniques, the ninja pushes herself to the point of pain to accomplish her goal.

Reactions   The reflexes and reactions of the ninja are honed to the sharpest possible edge.

Silence   The ninja does not brag or make a show of force. She seldom attacks without provocation. She kills only in self-defense.

Regarding the practice of these deadly and terrifying techniques, it should be noted that extreme care must be exercised. Most of these methods, using leverage, balance, and vital and fatal points, are so effective that even a near miss can put an opponent down or injure a training partner.

I recommend using pillows, cushions, mattresses, and so on to practice the striking techniques. In this way, the blows can be experienced with full force, making it possible for the defender to gauge their effectiveness. These are inexpensive and easily take the place of heavy bags, gloves, headgear, and the like. They are also often used in self-defense classes. Other schools employ a heavily padded attacker upon whom the defender may vent her anger and aggression, both of which are developed through training. Again, this requires someone willing to be knocked around and stomped, even though within the foam body armor the chance of injury is slight.

The best practice is with a willing male volunteer—your spouse, boyfriend, or friend. He must be sincere, not just out to show you how useless any such effort would be, since it takes a bit of time to experiment and make sure a technique is practiced correctly. "Low and slow" is the advice given to beginning wrestlers, and the same applies here. You should exert only enough pressure or resistance to initiate the technique. And, as above, care must be taken that you, as the student, do not accidentally injure him.

With time, speed and skill develop, and you can enjoy "flowery combat," practicing wrestling without injury.

2

ESCAPING FROM UNDERNEATH

Dragon Lady training begins with escaping from underneath. Women, typically less aggressive than men, often find themselves in a predicament before finding the will to resist.

These techniques may be useful in escaping a rapist or an abusive suitor. This aspect of the training system is taught first for psychological purposes, to build self-esteem and to overcome the cultural stereotype of submissiveness. Hence the title of this chapter, "Escaping From Underneath," a method of empowering the Dragon Lady to free herself from any sort of domination and take control of her fate.

The techniques for fighting on the ground are many, and it is best that the battle not rely on such tactics. However, if the enemy is much larger than the kunoichi, or if an aptitude for this type of strategy is demonstrated, the following basic principles and examples will help with escapes and reversals.

BASIC ESCAPE TECHNIQUES

If one is taken down to the ground, the first thing to do is to turn onto one's stomach. First, this prevents a pinning combination, and second, it sets up the countertechniques. All of the following practice forms begin in the "referee's position," in which both participants are on their hands and knees. This is known as the four-point stance. These four points, and the neck, form the five points of support for the mat-fighting set.

The attacker crouches beside the kunoichi with one arm around her waist and his outer hand holding her wrist. In actual combat, this is a transitory position, since the attacker must quickly consolidate his advantage to prevent the victim from escaping. Likewise, the kunoichi must seize the opportunity to employ the escaping or reversing movements, since she may have only one chance before the conflict advances to a more difficult stage.

Escape by Posting the Arm

Ideally, conflict should be resolved by the Dragon Lady before it becomes necessary to employ ground-fighting techniques.

FIGURE 15

FIGURE 16

FIGURE 17

However, in the event that the combatants grapple on the ground, "posting" one of the four points of support, a hand or a knee, is a means to facilitate an escape (Figure 15).

The Dragon Lady steps out with her right leg and swings her right arm up and back, preparing to throw her body weight out from under the enemy's arm, as if to land on her back (Figure 16). Normally this would be prevented by the secondary hold on her wrist.

Instead of falling on her back, the kunoichi simultaneously throws her right arm over the body of the enemy, twists her hips and shoulders over, and kicks out with her left leg. Placing her hand on the floor, she breaks his elbow against her body (Figure 17).

Escape by Turning In to the Enemy

From the all-fours stance, the Dragon Lady posts her right, outside leg and sets herself for a quick escape from the restraining hold the enemy has secured around her waist (Figure 18). Pivoting on her left knee and pushing off strongly with her right leg, she ducks her head and turns underneath the enemy's chest, pulling herself free of his grip (Figure 19). By rocking back on her heels, it is possible for her to gain enough distance between herself and the adversary to extricate herself completely from his grasp (Figure 20).

Side Roll Escape

The attacker has secured a hold on the kunoichi's waist and wrist (Figure 21). Due to his forward position, it would be difficult to turn in to him. So the Dragon Lady takes advantage of her own hold and weight to reverse the situation.

Taking a firm grip on the enemy's wrist with her right hand, she pulls her knees together as she strikes up into her attacker's chest with her left elbow and rolls to her right (Figure 22). As the opponent falls on his back, the kunoichi follows through by dri-

FIGURE 18

FIGURE 19

FIGURE 20

FIGURE 21

FIGURE 22

FIGURE 23

ving her elbow into his chin, knocking him out before he can recover (Figure 23).

Sit-out Escape

The most basic escape technique of the kunoichi is the sit-out escape. From the kneeling position, she posts her right leg to ready herself for the movement that will wrench her free of the enemy's hold on her waist and wrist (Figure 24). Throwing her right arm up and over, the Dragon Lady throws her left leg out from under the enemy's grip. The momentum enables her to achieve enough distance to make a successful escape (Figure 25). Pivoting on her right knee as she comes around behind the enemy, she entwines her right arm around his neck, letting the inertia of her left arm pull her behind him for the takedown and choke hold (Figure 26).

FIGURE 24

FIGURE 25

FIGURE 26

GROUND FIGHTING

Naturally, it is best if the kunoichi can accomplish her mission and return to friendly territory without incident. While every precaution is taken and every contingency is considered to insure the safety and security of the operation and the agent, occasions arise when it becomes necessary to engage in combat with the enemy. At those times, the faster he can be overcome, the better. Therefore the Dragon Lady trains in the martial arts, knowing that if she's caught or captured, it is unlikely that help will arrive in time. Due to the greater strength of most of her adversaries, special techniques are best suited to the female agent. Among these are the ancient art of *sutemi-jitsu*, or fighting as the underdog.

In the event the kunoichi is thrown to the ground, or if she should choose to make the enemy lose his superior (higher) position by bending forward, she must first assume a defensive position by directing her shoulder toward the enemy, drawing both elbows in to protect the ribs and bringing the knees in slightly. As shown in Figure 27, she uses them as a base to check the enemy's advance by blocking his ankle with her feet. This presents the smallest target to the enemy and gives the appearance of helplessness.

As shown in Figure 28, she bends the left knee more closely to the chest and strikes out strongly with a powerful side kick to the enemy's groin, abdomen, or solar plexus with her heel. Some schools teach the blade kick, which uses the edge of the foot. Our purpose, however, is to drive the enemy back as well as strike one of his vital or fatal points.

The Dragon Lady then deftly rolls onto her back (Figure 29) and crosses her arms defensively in front of her. Her hands form tiger claw fists, to be used if necessary. She then strikes upward with the heel of her right foot to deliver a snap kick to the enemy's chin, which has been brought into range by the first strike to his centerline. Obviously, this technique could also be directed against the enemy's groin or solar plexus.

FIGURE 27

FIGURE 28

FIGURE 29

FIGURE 30

To set up the coup de grâce, the Dragon Lady shifts back to her right side and drives a side kick into the enemy's knee (Figure 30). This knee strike may likewise be used as an attack when the enemy approaches. However, if it is used too soon he might not come into range for the other strikes. With this technique, the purpose is to break his balance as well as his leg.

To finish the enemy off, the kunoichi grabs the enemy's arm or lapel and pulls him down on top of her. He cannot fall straight down, however, since his left leg is blocked or jammed. Instead, by continuing to roll to her right and blocking his leg, the Dragon Lady drops the enemy on his face. Springing up, or coming up on one knee as the enemy topples over, completes her escape.

Turning the Tables by Breaking the Elbow

Fighting on the ground is an area of martial combat which is often neglected in practice, yet is essential for the art to be considered complete. The ninja have a wide variety of such techniques, and many of them are particularly suited to the kunoichi, or female agent. If the enemy is a superior fighter or if he is stronger and overpowering, one may find oneself in what is referred to in wrestling as a predicament, that is, the female is in imminent danger of being pinned and losing the match. At such a moment, the skillful kunoichi must act swiftly, for she is playing the game of life and death, and losing a fall may mean losing her life. Naturally, in the training hall, one must practice slowly to avoid injuring one's partner, but even the moderate amount of pressure called for here will convince all doubters of the efficacy of this technique when applied with force and vigor, as would be called for in self-defense.

In Figure 31, the enemy has thrown the agent to the mat, or she has been rendered unconscious and awakens to find herself pinned, as shown. The enemy may be choking with one hand or simply twisting the face to the side in a gesture of power. In

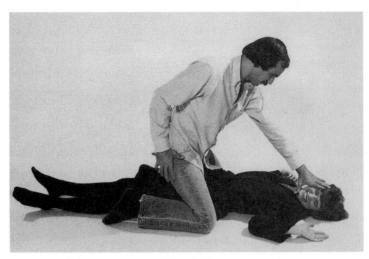

FIGURE 31

either case, his extended arm is the target. It matters little if he has both hands at the throat, since that just means there are two arms to break instead of one.

Reaching across with her left hand, the kunoichi takes hold of the enemy's wrist to relieve the pressure and make sure he doesn't draw back and get away (Figure 32). At the same time, she drives her right forearm, or hammer fist, into the back of the enemy's elbow. This "snaps" the elbow and often breaks the joint by hyperextending it.

She takes advantage of the enemy by tilting to his right and jerking her right foot in. This action helps throw the enemy to his right by jacking his left leg off the floor. Simultaneously, she pushes against the shattered left elbow with the heel of her right hand and quickly rotates her hips to the left. This throws the enemy to the side. He may try to save himself by posting his right hand out to the side as he feels himself go over. Should this occur, she simply reaches out with her left hand and sweeps it out from under him so he falls, as desired.

As the enemy falls on his right shoulder (Figure 33), she

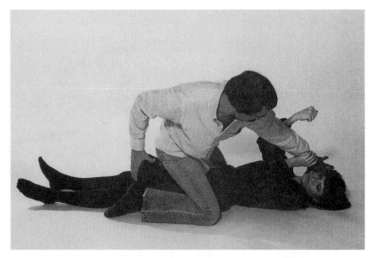

FIGURE 32

FIGURE 33

quickly rolls onto her knees and takes advantage of his momentum to throw him on his back. Then she places her right knee
against his stomach and presses the air out of him while reaching forward and strangling him with his collar, or she finishes
him by using the heel stomp to the face or chest.

Turning the Tables by Pulling the Elbow Through

From time to time, the kunoichi may use her feminine wiles to lead the enemy on. In such a case, the agent may find herself beneath the enemy but not yet in immediate danger. Reversing the situation and regaining control depends largely on balance and surprise to be wholly successful.

Figure 34 shows that the enemy has reached a position in which he straddles the kunoichi's hips. He leans forward on his left arm, confident of his position, and begins a secondary attack with his right hand. The Dragon Lady forestalls this movement by catching his right hand in her left. If this were an assault, she would also deliver a palm heel strike to the enemy's chin to drive him upward and help break his balance, but since she is only "checkmating" the enemy's movements rather than fighting for her life, the agent slides her fingers down the outside of the enemy's left arm and locates the larger muscle on top of his forearm.

The Dragon Lady then bends the enemy's elbow by reaching inside with her fingers or thumb and pressing against the ten-

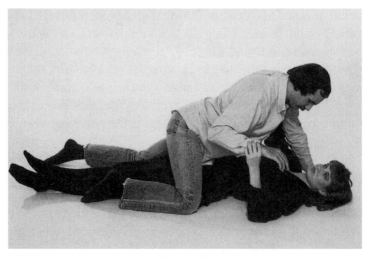

FIGURE 34

FIGURE 35

dons in the crook of the elbow (Figure 35). Alternatively, she could bring her hand inside the elbow and bend it outward by pushing against the tendons with the edge of her hand. This makes the enemy lose his balance, tipping forward, and he reacts by trying to straighten up. At the same time, the Dragon Lady snaps her right knee upward to lift the enemy off his left side. In combat, this strike would be stronger and higher, directed at the groin. Simultaneously, she pulls the enemy's arm across the line of engagement to throw him even further off balance. (The line of engagement is an imaginary line drawn between the solar plexuses of two combatants. It indicates the path of any straight-forward attack. Other attacks are said to cross this line or parallel it. Basically, the line of engagement is the space between two fighters.)

As the enemy falls to the right, she rolls onto her left hip and lightly pins him by both shoulders. This is not a hard fall, so it is unlikely that the enemy will be rendered senseless by it, yet it is sufficient to momentarily take him aback due to the sudden loss of balance and the natural fear of falling (Figure 36). It is really a

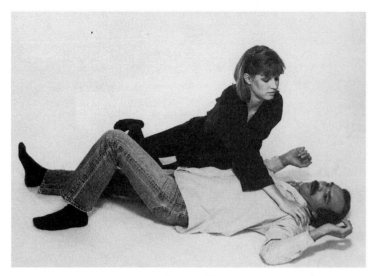

FIGURE 36

gentle roll, which keeps the enemy from saving himself by reaching out with his free hand when his left arm is bent. The action may be enough to prevent a more forceful attack.

In combat, of course, once the previous stage had been reached the kunoichi would retain control of the enemy's wrist while pulling his arm through. When he hits the ground, she continues his roll as before, so he ends up on his back. She quickly stands, twisting and locking his right arm, before executing a heel stomp kick to the face or throat.

3

BREAKING THE BALANCE

In ninjitsu, we often speak about breaking the enemy's balance. This means that the enemy must be made to fall over, which may be accomplished by many methods, but here we shall speak of the simplest.

Between the feet there exists an imaginary line, known as the line of balance, which represents the strongest part of the enemy's foundation. A person can resist far more pressure when it is directed in a straight line against his shoulder from the side. This is because the force is acting against the resistance of both of the legs. On the other hand, when the enemy stands with his feet shoulder-width apart, toes pointing directly forward, a gentle push against his chest will easily topple him backward. This is because the only resistance is the grip of the feet. Such a force acts perpendicular to the enemy's line of balance rather than parallel to it. These principles are the basis for all throwing techniques.

Against a larger and more powerful opponent, the Dragon Lady must employ such subtle tricks as breaking the balance, since the object is to bring the enemy down to size. *Judoka* are taught many feints and techniques for determining to which angle the enemy is vulnerable, but these take years of practice and require a variety of throws to take advantage of the subtle shifts in the center of gravity.

Knee Chop

For the application of this technique, the kunoichi may position herself by slide-stepping forward or by letting the enemy advance and seemingly push her off balance to the rear. Then she lifts her right heel up and behind the enemy's left calf (Figure 37).

In Figure 38, the Dragon Lady strikes downward with the back of her heel, intending to rupture the muscle on the back of the shin or tear the ligaments and blood vessels behind the knee. Do not be afraid to strike repeatedly. Break the enemy's leg from behind if need be. This attack will force him to lift his leg to save it from the punishing blows, at which point it may be swept across the line of engagement by a scooping kick with the right

FIGURE 37

FIGURE 38

FIGURE 39

foot. Alternatively, the leg may be broken down from the front. If so, when the knee hits the ground, stamp firmly on the enemy's upraised heel. This will rip the Achilles tendon off the bone of his heel and permanently cripple him. Bearing in mind the enemy's *kuzushi*, or balance, when his foot is lifted off the floor, push against his right arm with your left hand and pull on his left arm with your right. This shoulder-twisting action contributes to toppling him still further.

In Figure 39, the Dragon Lady pulls the enemy over through her hold on his left arm and retains control of him with that grip. When properly executed, this throw drops the enemy soundly on his back, effectively driving the wind out of his lungs. Once he is down, he can be quickly and easily disposed of.

Foot Sweep

A more subtle application of the same principle is the simple foot sweep. It does, of course, require considerably more practice and good timing. In Figure 40, the enemy and Dragon Lady have "tied up." She has grasped both of his arms and pressed into the hollow of each elbow to halt his advance. At the same time, she steps to the outside of his left foot with her right foot. As the enemy shifts his weight to the right in an effort to escape from the numbing elbow grip (Figure 41), his weight is off his left leg. The Dragon Lady then pushes with her left hand and pulls with her right to twist the enemy to his right rear corner. With her right foot, she scoops his left foot out from under him. The enemy crashes to the mat, where he can be finished off with a heel stomp to the head or chest, as shown in Figure 42.

Bear Hug Escape (Front)

The attacker secures a front waist cinch and begins to apply crushing pressure. This is the classic bear hug attack (Figure 43). (Beyond the likelihood of internal injuries, such a hold can suffocate the victim into unconsciousness in about two minutes.)

FIGURE 40

FIGURE 41

FIGURE 42

Immediately bring both hands to the attacker's face and position your thumbs over his eyes. Hook your fingers behind his ears and in his hair for a firmer grip (Figure 44). Tense the entire body and drive your thumbs into the enemy's eyes (Figure 45). This will produce sufficient pain to ensure your release, because the instinctive reaction is to bring the hands to the face, which necessitates release of the hold.

Naturally, any attack to the eyes must be used only as a last resort, since there is an excellent chance the attacker will be permanently blinded.

Bear Hug Escape (Behind)

The attacker has seized the Dragon Lady from behind with a waist cinch and locked his hands to secure the hold (Figure 46). Pretending to submit to the embrace, she offers little resistance,

FIGURE 43

FIGURE 44

FIGURE 45

FIGURE 46

FIGURE 47

FIGURE 48

aware that the more she fights, the more pressure he will exert, forcing the air out of her lungs.

The kunoichi waits until the attacker is sufficiently relaxed or until he has gained enough confidence to change position. Then she steps to the left and drives the point of her elbow into his solar plexus (Figure 47).

Immediately following up on her advantage, she secures her release from the encircling hold and whips back and upward from the elbow with a right vertical back fist to strike the attacker squarely on the nose (Figure 48). This will cause his eyes to water uncontrollably, as well as numb his face.

Groin Rip

When the attacker stands to one side slightly behind the Dragon Lady, as when she has released herself from the bear hug just described, it is often advantageous to disable the attacker more permanently with a strike to his groin. The target is the

FIGURE 49

FIGURE 50

FIGURE 51

pubic arch, which unites the front halves of the pelvis. This thin strip of bone is fairly easily broken with a firm strike of the edge of the hand. *Kiai* (spirit-shout) as the strike is delivered (Figure 49). This adds impact and energy to the attack.

To complete the technique, seize the attacker's genitals by reaching up and back with an inverted tiger claw fist and pull him forward with this pressure on his groin (Figure 50).

Throat Lock Escape

Even in the most desperate circumstances, with her hands tied and the enemy's hand on her throat (Figure 51), the Dragon Lady is not without recourse or escape. The first step is to relieve the crushing pressure against the throat by dropping the chin to the chest. This tenses the muscles of the neck, making it harder to grip, and forms a protected area for the windpipe, or trachea. Next, grab the attacker's wrist with both hands, thumbs against

FIGURE 52

FIGURE 53

the attacker's palm. Twist away from the hand by turning the shoulders and head to one side (Figure 52). Using the wristlock, bend the attacker forward by directing pressure against his elbow and proceed with the takedown (Figure 53).

Side Headlock Escape

When grappling with an opponent, the attacker may gain the upper hand by slipping an arm around the neck of his victim and seizing his own wrist, thus forming a side headlock hold (Figure 54).

Normally, pressure from this grip would soon compel submission or suffocation, but the Dragon Lady can reverse the situation by cupping the enemy's chin with her left hand as her hand comes up over his right shoulder. At the same time, she turns in to the hold with her head to relieve pressure against her throat and pulls

FIGURE 54

FIGURE 55

FIGURE 56

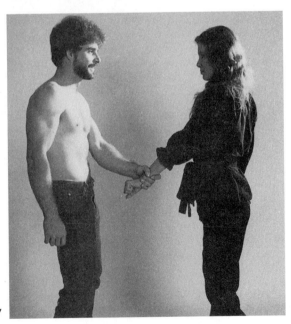

FIGURE 57

on the enemy's thumb to break his grip. Her left knee then digs into his knee to prevent him from stepping away (Figure 55).

By using leverage against his chin, or by raking his nose or pulling his hair, the kunoichi bends the enemy over backward, breaking his balance. Then, leaning back to direct her knee into his support leg, she pounds on his chest with a hammer fist (Figure 56). Targets include the solar plexus, belly, and groin.

Wrist Grab Release

For this demonstration, imagine that the attacker and the Dragon Lady have engaged in a verbal exchange and that she, seeking to avoid a confrontation, has started to turn and walk away. The attacker reaches out and uses a normal overhand grip on her wrist to prevent her from moving (Figure 57). Remembering the principle of yielding, the kunoichi pushes forward slightly with her trapped wrist, thus inducing the attacker to stop or slacken his grip. This technique also works well against any cross grip by the attacker before he can push or, more likely, *pull* the victim toward him.

As the attacker begins to react, the Dragon Lady immediately reverses her direction and swings her hand, palm facing the attacker, in a small counterclockwise circle at the solar plexus level. The leverage of the wrists binding against each other will free her hand of the hold. She now reverses the hold by slapping down on the attacker's wrist and encircling it with her fingers (Figure 58). By quickly pulling forward along a line perpendicular to his line of balance, she can tip over and throw the enemy.

Elbow Takedown

Whenever the Dragon Lady has a firm grip on the enemy's wrist, as in the release from a wrist grab, she may take the opportunity to manipulate his arm and defeat him with a simple takedown.

Bend the captured wrist so the back of the hand faces down.

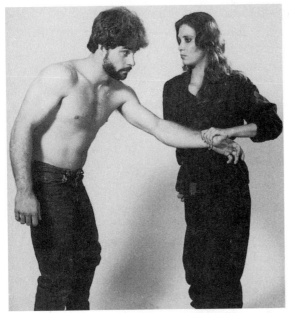

FIGURE 58

FIGURE 59

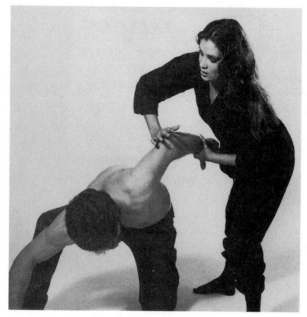

FIGURE 60

The attacker will react by pulling back, trying to free his arm. Seize the chance to break his balance by allowing the arm to bend at the elbow, forming a 90 degee angle. Then place the heel of your right hand against the joint and push forward (Figure 59). This action produces excruciating pressure and is likely to dislocate the elbow joint if sufficient pressure is applied. Your attacker will instinctively bend forward; when he does this, merely direct the push of the hand down to bring the attacker under control (Figure 60).

Handshake Escape

Upon an introduction, a young lady may find the new acquaintance reluctant to relinquish the hold on her hand (Figure 61). The kunoichi has a simple means of dealing with such a situation, which can also be effective when combatants are engaged right hand to right hand. Furthermore, should an

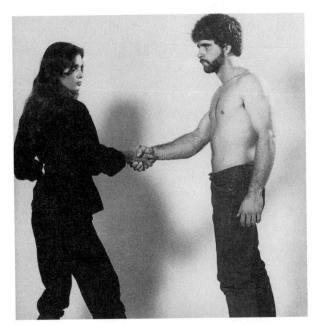

FIGURE 61

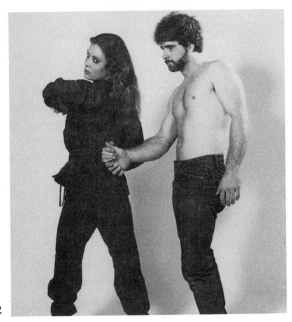

FIGURE 62

FIGURE 63

attacker succeed in twisting your arm behind your back, this strike is excellent as a preparatory movement.

Pivot on both heels simultaneously without trying to pull our hand free. This will "wrap" your right arm behind you, while the left arm is loaded at shoulder level (Figure 62). Step back with your left foot to close the gap between yourself and the attacker. Using the momentum of the spin, strike up and back with your left elbow to the carotid plexus, just below the earlobe (Figure 63). A sharp blow at this point will stun the opponent.

Spinning Back Fist

On occasion, the Dragon Lady will use her wiles to lure the enemy in for a hit. One such example is use of the spinning back fist. At times, a gentleman may be called upon to demonstrate respect for his hostess by taking her hand (Figure 64). Or, she

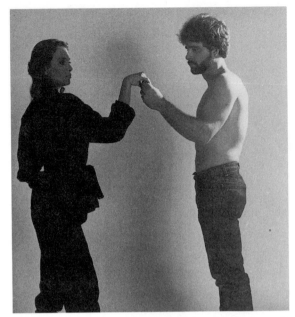

FIGURE 64

FIGURE 65

may attract his attention to her ring or bracelet. The kunoichi of old called this technique "leading down the path."

Once the attacker has your hand, pivot on the ball of the right foot and swing your left leg in a wide arc to the outside. Using the dance technique of "pointing," turn your head more quickly than your shoulders to look behind you and sight-in on the target. Whip your closed left fist in a horizontal arc at shoulder level, snapping out with the wrist to strike the attacker directly on the left temple with the first two knuckles of your outstretched hand (Figure 65). To accurately gauge the distance to the target, you may retain your hold on the fingers of the attacker. This strike is usually sufficient to render the victim unconscious.

4

TAKING OFF THE HAND

The human hand, with its complexity and dexterity, is by far one of the most incredible feats of engineering and functionality ever created. Because of this, one has a natural tendency to protect it; the hand also gives the kunoichi access to many very sensitive nerves, small ligaments, and muscles of the enemy.

Finger Ripping

The weakest point of the hand is the webbing between the middle and ring fingers. These two digits are operated from the wrist by the same tendon and therefore tend to move in unison. By gripping two of the enemy's fingers in each hand and spreading them apart, pain can be made to radiate all the way up to the enemy's neck via the brachial nerve. Once this pull is applied, the enemy will most likely try to jerk his hand away. Control him by his fingers and throw him to the ground, where he can be pinned or given the coup de grâce (Figure 66).

Another ancient trick involves ripping the fingers apart (Figure 67). Pulling up and to the left on the index and middle fingers and down to the right with the ring and little fingers

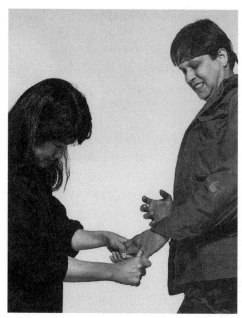

FIGURE 66

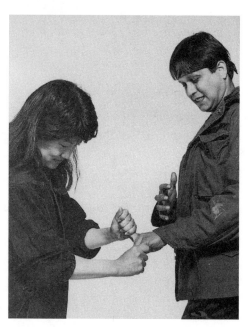

FIGURE 67

tears the hand apart. Permanent injury may result from even a mild application of this technique.

Finally, any single finger may be injured by hyperextending or flexing it. Although this is not as fast a method as spreading or ripping, it is effective.

Kotegoshi (Wristlock)

Wristlocks are exotic methods of breaking the enemy's balance. They take advantage of the particular arrangement of the numerous multifaceted carpal bones of the wrist and the two long bones of the forearm to exert pressure not only against the fingers but the wrist and elbow as well. The shoulder is involved as a secondary complication of the twisting action. The *kotegoshi* is applied by placing both thumbs in the center of the back of the enemy's hand and then gripping the large muscles at the base of the thumb and the little finger by curling your fingers around the attacker's hand. Bend the hand, palm side toward the inside of the elbow (Figure 68), to effect the lock. When sufficient force is applied, the fingers are pushed back toward the shoulder and the enemy can be pushed downward to the mat.

Nikkyo (Wristlock)

Like *kotegoshi*, *nikkyo* is applied by placing the thumbs in the center of the back of the hand and gripping the sides of the palm with the fingers. In this lock, however, the fingers point downward instead of up. The pressure is applied by bending the palm side of the hand toward the back of the elbow (Figure 69). Once in place, either wristlock may then be employed, describing a clockwise circle with the arm. By these means, the arm can be twisted, or "turned over." This locks the elbow and involves the shoulder. Such total involvement of the limb invariably produces intense pain and enables the Dragon Lady to subdue even a larger or more powerful opponent.

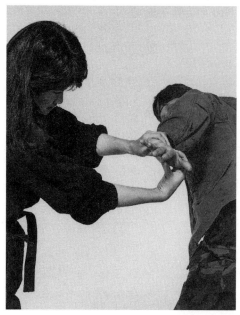

FIGURE 68

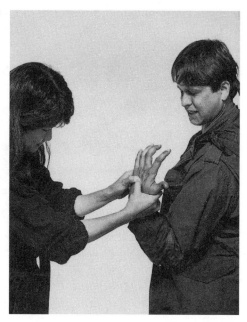

FIGURE 69

Taking the Elbow to the High Inside

The wrist release is one of the most fundamental escape techniques and is taught in almost every school of self-defense. When executed to the outside of the enemy's wrist, it enables the kunoichi to employ the very painful *nikkyo* wristlock. It must be applied quickly and can then be used to take the enemy to the mat. In practice, be extremely careful not to injure your partner!

In Figure 70, the enemy grips the Dragon Lady's wrist with his right hand, intending to prevent her escape or to take her prisoner. The initial reaction of most people is to pull away. Not so the Dragon Lady. Instead, she may push forward, causing the enemy to stop pulling so hard because he is being effective. This is the setup.

In Figure 71, the kunoichi straightens the fingers of her right hand and swings her wrist in a small clockwise arc. Since the enemy's wrist was relaxed by the previous feint, the agent's

FIGURE 70

FIGURE 71

FIGURE 72

FIGURE 73

hand has sufficient momentum to swing outside his wrist. The leverage of this action jerks the hand free of the encircling grip by acting against the little-finger side of the hand. Once she has released herself, the kunoichi continues to circle and reverses the grip, capturing the enemy's wrist and slightly turning over his arm. This effect can be enhanced by pulling down on the attacker's arm to lock the elbow while the wrist is twisted.

In Figure 72, the Dragon Lady slides her hand down the enemy's arm to his wrist. Her thumb and forefinger encircle his wrist while the rest of the fingers press against the back of his hand, bending his fingers, palm up, toward the back of his elbow. At the same time, she drives the heel of her left hand against the enemy's elbow to break the joint and twist the arm still further. The leverage of this technique can easily dislocate the shoulder anteriorly.

FIGURE 74

In Figure 73, the Dragon Lady increases the severity of the pain in the enemy's arm by lifting his trapped wrist straight upward and continuing to press forward on his elbow with her other hand. This hold could easily be slipped behind the enemy's back and turned into a hammer lock, but this is not an easy hold for a woman to maintain, and the enemy might escape and renew his attack. Therefore, the kunoichi steps forward with her left foot and places her leg in front of his right leg in order to trip him. Through the pushing and lifting action on his arm, the painful wristlock, and a forward throw, the enemy falls to his right front corner (Figure 74). The impact will dislocate his shoulder, if it had not done so previously, and he can be finished off with a knee strike to the head.

Taking Off the Hand to the High Outside

Should the enemy seize your right wrist with his right hand, thus crossing the line of engagement with his own arm, take advantage of this opportunity to apply the very painful *kote-goshi* wristlock. In the ancient jujitsu texts, such techniques were

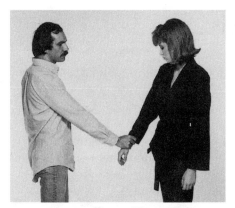

FIGURE 75

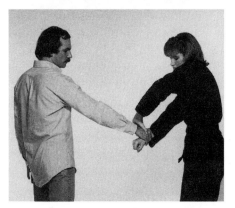

FIGURE 76

FIGURE 77

referred to as "taking off the hand," and this designation has been retained in most of the ninjitsu schools.

The basic action of the *kotegoshi* movement is to twist the little-finger side of the hand toward the thumb side of the wrist. Since the enemy's arm is between the combatants, most of the effectiveness of his left arm has been neutralized. Because of the sudden pain in his wrist, the enemy finds that his hand is easily carried up toward his right shoulder, thus breaking his balance to his right front corner.

In Figure 75, the enemy is reaching forward and taking hold of the kunoichi's right wrist with his right hand. This might occur if she were trying to leave against his wishes or if she were reaching forward.

In Figure 76, the kunoichi reaches over with the fingers of her left hand to seize the large muscle at the base of the enemy's thumb, placing the ball of her left thumb in the center back of the enemy's hand. If the kunoichi is using the lazy poison hand, she may elect to stab her thumbnail into the back of the hand at this point and "inject" the victim with the toxin she carries under a sharpened thumbnail. Further, if the enemy tries to block this action because it is not done swiftly enough, the Dragon Lady need only pivot on the heel of her left foot and drive her forearm against the enemy's elbow to break his hold, and elbow.

Next, she pulls up and back using her grip on the base of the enemy's thumb and wrenches his arm out past his right shoulder (Figure 77). (When practicing this, be careful to go slowly lest you injure your partner.) In combat, when the snapping action of the *kotegoshi* wristlock is applied in this manner, the many bones of the wrist quickly dislocate, causing intense pain and effectively breaking the wrist. By this action, the enemy is made to lean to his right.

Figure 78 shows how the Dragon Lady pivots 180 degrees on the heel of her left foot, pulling the enemy around to her left rear corner. Remember, in combat this is one smooth and dynamic movement; the enemy must follow the wristlock and take the fall or his elbow, and then shoulder, will dislocate. Once he

FIGURE 78

lands, finish him off with a heel stomp to the throat or face. Maintain control of his wrist and arm all the way down to forestall any type of counterattack, and if necessary, be ready to trip the enemy with your left leg as you throw.

Taking Off the Hand to the Low Outside

An application of the *kotegoshi* wristlock, which is highly effective in disabling the enemy, may be used when he is foolish enough to seize your right hand with his left. Since the line of engagement between the combatants is clear, that is, the enemy is free to strike with his other arm unless the kunoichi presents a secondary defense, it is advisable for the agent to move quickly to the outside line in order to regain control of the situation and forestall any further aggression.

If the enemy aggressively reaches forward and grabs the kunoichi's left hand, she should quickly lower her center for a

FIGURE 79

FIGURE 80

firmer base of support and balance. Reaching over with the fingers of her left hand, she forms a countergrip on the muscle on the little-finger side of the enemy's hand, placing the ball of her thumb in the center of the back of the enemy's hand (Figure 79). With this grip, it is possible to "peel away" the enemy's hand with pressure against the metacarpal bones and the leverage that the hold provides. If the enemy steps forward to counter this action, the kunoichi pivots on the heel of her right foot and swings out to the rear with her left leg. This takes her to the outside and drives her right hip against the enemy's left elbow, breaking his hold and freeing her hand.

Figure 80 shows how she pulls the enemy's arm out straight as she "takes off" his hand, lifting in a circular motion up and out. This locks the enemy elbow and, due to the severe pain of the *kotegoshi* wristlock, makes the enemy bend at the waist to relieve the pressure. In combat, this action is very fast and normally snaps the elbow before sufficient pressure can be directed against the wrist to make it break first. If the enemy should try to counter by shifting forward and bending his arm, use this advantage position to strike down on his elbow with your new free right hand. Aim the blow squarely at the joint and make contact with the hammer fist strike. This will induce the enemy

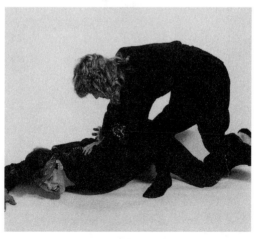

FIGURE 81

to cooperate, but by breaking his elbow and his balance toward his right front corner.

Then, pivot on the ball of your right foot to swing behind the enemy while keeping control of his arm with the wristlock and augmenting an elbow bar (Figure 81). If necessary, be prepared to trip him over your right leg to take him down. Once he falls onto his chest and face, he may be pinned by pressing his extended arm to the floor using the wrist/elbow hold, or he may be finished off by striking the base of the skull with the edge of the hand strike.

Taking the Elbow to the Low Inside

Hairstyles have radically changed over the years, but generally speaking, women wear their hair longer than men. Therefore, some consideration must be given to an attack to this vulnerable target. A handful of hair provides a good grip and, at least initially, provides a great deal of control over the victim due to the pain inflicted. However, within a few seconds, the scalp numbs itself so the primary difficulty comes from the leverage this hold provides for jerking the head about. It is virtually impossible to make the enemy let go of hair quickly even if he were so inclined; his fingers, rings, or jewelry may become entangled. It matters little if the hair is worn long and is grabbed near the end or is short and gripped near the scalp. The first thing that must be done is to nullify the hold.

Figure 82 shows the enemy reaching forward and grabbing the Dragon Lady's hair in an attempt to capture her or prevent her escape. She no longer attempts to flee but turns her attention toward the enemy. She bends both knees slightly to lower her center of gravity and ensure her balance. Then both arms begin to come up defensively.

In Figure 83, the kunoichi reaches up with both hands and takes hold of the enemy's hand and wrist. If possible, she presses his hand to her scalp in an effort to flatten out his fingers. She may also employ the finger ripping technique to open his hand, or try to dislocate his thumb by pulling it back toward his wrist.

FIGURE 82

FIGURE 83

In any event, by these means she now has control of the enemy rather than the other way around. Make no mistake, the Dragon Lady must act quickly and take the enemy by surprise to be effective. She then turns her left side toward him to present the smallest possible target and lifts her left leg to "chamber" her sidekick.

The Dragon Lady strikes out strongly with the heel of her left foot (Figure 84), driving into the enemy's groin, stomach, or solar plexus. But he cannot get away because she still has his hand. His hold is no longer effective, and the wind is knocked out of him through the dynamic action of the kick. The Dragon Lady maintains her balance by holding the enemy, while his balance is broken forward by the strike. Taking the enemy's hand off her hair, the kunoichi applies the extremely painful *nikkyo* wristlock, which turns the enemy's arm over and locks his elbow against her left shoulder (Figure 85). The *nikkyo* technique twists

FIGURE 84

FIGURE 85

FIGURE 86

the enemy's thumb toward the little-finger side of his hand. Then the kunoichi pulls the enemy's arm down and diagonally across the line of engagement, further destroying his balance to his right front corner, and begins to turn her hips clockwise to add her weight to the throw. In the event the enemy tried to step forward and save himself, she could block his right ankle with her left leg.

Figure 86 shows the enemy driven forward onto his face and pinned to the mat by the pressure against his locked right elbow. In this position, the elbow or shoulder can be broken, or the enemy finished off with the appropriate technique.

Breaking the Finger to the Rear

There are several methods which enable the kunoichi to effect a release in the unlikely event that the enemy should succeed insecuring a "cinching hold." This situation might occur if one-faces multiple attackers or steps through a doorway without checking for someone lurking just inside. In the most difficult instance, the arms are pinned to the sides by the encircling hold. Regardless of whether the enemy has secured this hold by surprise or due to superior numbers, it is imperative that the agent escape to a safe position as quickly as possible. In this case, she will reverse the hold during her escape, and either place the enemy in front of her as a human shield or take him down from behind.

Figure 87 shows the enemy attacking with a rear bear hug, which traps the agent's arms at her sides above the elbow. The Dragon Lady immediately bends both knees slightly to lower her center of gravity for better stability. At the same time, she exhales and performs the "silent *kiai*" to tense her body and prepare for movement.

If necessary, the kunoichi digs her nails into the back of the enemy's hand to secure a grip on one or more fingers. In this presentation, the little-finger break is employed. Another method for loosening the enemy's grip is to grind one of the knuckles into the back of the enemy's hand. At this point there are many secondary strikes which can be applied: striking the enemy's nose with the back of your head; stomping on his instep with your heel; or reaching behind to grab him in the groin.

In Figure 88, by causing intense pain in the enemy's hand, the kunoichi breaks his grip and then pivots 180 degrees to the left rear, maintaining a secure hold on the finger as she turns to the outside line. This may be done by augmenting the finger lock with the other hand or by striking the enemy's elbow with the right hand. Then she pivots a second 180 degrees on the heel of the left foot and strikes the enemy's shoulder from behind with the heel of her right palm. If he steps forward in an attempt to escape (Figure 89), she bends her left knee and strikes the side of his left knee as he steps. This "breakdown," plus the pushing action on the shoulder and the finger lock, compels the enemy to bend over and drop to his knee. If this movement is performed swiftly, the knee break will not be needed, since the arm bar alone can do the trick. Having now turned 360 degrees and brought the enemy in front (Figure 90), she pushes forward and down on his shoulder, driving him to the ground to knock the wind out of him. Once he is down, she presses against his left

FIGURE 87

FIGURE 88

FIGURE 89

FIGURE 90

calf with her right knee and pins him with the arm bar and the punishing leg hold.

Bearing Down by the Double Wristlock

The enemy may seize the kunoichi in such a way that a wristhold is impossible and no evasive steps may be easily taken, as when her back is to a wall. On occasions when the enemy feels confident of his control of the situation, he may penetrate more deeply into the sphere of influence of the female ninja, thus bringing about his own undoing. This technique takes advantage of a subtle hold on both wrists, but the wristlock may be applied with equal effectiveness on a single wrist, or by pressing the enemy's hand against one arm with the opposite hand.

With the combatants face to face, the enemy reaches forward and secures a hold on both arms at the elbow. Naturally, every attempt should be made to prevent this from happening, by blocking, stepping away, or fending off the attack using whatever means are available. In this presentation, the enemy grip is above the elbow, but the movement works just as well when his hands are further down on the forearms or even when gripping both wrists from above.

In Figure 91, the kunoichi quickly wraps both of her arms over the enemy's forearms, thereby trapping his hands in the crook of each elbow. In this illustration, the fingers lie on the biceps and the metacarpal bones of the hands are squeezed by the elbow joint. If your intention is merely to escape rather than catch his hands, beat down strongly with both hammer fists or forearms to break the radial bones of the enemy's forearms, striking directly downward on the center of the bone.

Then, hooking your hands together without interlocking the fingers, pull this double fist toward your centerline and downward. This reinforces the finger lock on the enemy's hands and

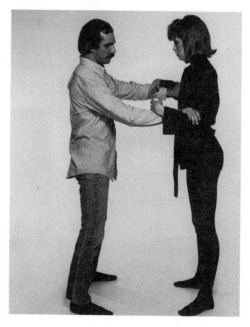

FIGURE 91

FIGURE 92

FIGURE 93

brings crushing pressure to his wrists, forcing him to bend his knees to relieve the pressure. Add to the pressure on his wrists by bending slightly forward and "bearing him down." If the enemy steps forward defensively, twist to either side and throw him down using a double armlock. If he tries to step back, hook either ankle and push him over backward.

By employing the double wristlock described, the enemy may easily be forced to his knees and made to abandon his attack. However, since it was his own attack that brought him to this state, and since it is unlikely that having the tables turned will sit very well with him, it is also unlikely that any plea of submission or surrender will be genuine. Therefore, the ninja and kunoichi are trained to deliver the coup de grâce whenever it becomes necessary to defend themselves. As the enemy is brought to his knees, she strikes strongly upward with her left knee, driving into the enemy's chin to disable and stun, if not kill, him (Figure 92).

Throwing by Entangling Both Arms (Front)

The following technique works equally well against a single-arm or lapel grip. In the training hall, it is usually practiced against an extended choke. Incidentally, since this strike depends largely on the action of breaking and locking the elbows, it could as easily be employed if the kunoichi were prone and the enemy choking from above. The impact against the arms would make him roll to one side, and he could then be thrown off so an escape could be effected. Alternatively, the Dragon Lady might take advantage of the sudden reversal in the situation and quickly kill the enemy.

Anytime a choke hold is obtained by the enemy, relief of the disabling pressure is the first thing to accomplish. This is done by bending the head forward as if to touch the chin to the chest (Figure 93). This flexes the sternocleiomastoideus muscles along the side of the neck, which protect the carotid artery, and pulls the trachea back into the hollow of the throat, making it more difficult for the enemy to direct pressure against it with his thumbs. Simultaneously bend both knees and lower your center of gravity for greater stability. Furthermore, these actions will later serve as the psychological trigger that will initiate the appropriate defensive response.

The kunoichi toes out with the right foot and swings the right arm out to the side to gather momentum, as shown in Figure 94. In a corollary action, she executes a little-finger break on the enemy's right hand with her left, or presses upward against his forearm to lock his elbow and make him think she is turning to the right.

She quickly pivots on the heels of both feet back to the left and drives down onto both of the enemy's arms with her whipping right arm (Figure 95). At the same time, she reverses her pull with the left hand to help turn the enemy and break his hold. Much of this technique is the power strike, but just as necessary are proper timing and deception so the enemy is feinted off balance and helps in his own downfall.

As shown in Figure 96, she pivots on the left foot and steps in front of the enemy's right foot with her own right foot. She then seizes his right wrist with her left hand and his right elbow with her right hand, trapping his left arm underneath her arms and against her body. Then she pulls him around and over her right hip, blocking his right leg with her right and toppling him forward and down.

As the enemy falls to the mat, the kunoichi bends her right knee and continues to turn to her left front corner (Figure 97). As the wind is knocked out of him, she maintains control of his right arm with her previous grip. As the enemy lands, she breaks his right arm by levering it over her left knee and stuns him with a hammer fist to the solar plexus or the side of the neck (Figure 98).

Throwing the Enemy by Entangling Both Arms (Rear)

In the dojo, or training hall, we still practice some techniques in the form of escapes, or reversals. One such tactic was devel-

FIGURE 94

FIGURE 95

FIGURE 96

FIGURE 97

FIGURE 98

oped as a defense against an attack in which the enemy obtains a hold on the neck from behind. This might occur if the enemy grabs the collar or takes hold of the hair from behind. Like the other methods illustrated here, the movements should be executed slowly and with some care until they are perfected. Be sure that your training partner knows how to fall safely, and advance to moderate speed only after considerable practice.

Figure 99 shows the enemy having secured a rear choke hold. The Dragon Lady counters by bending her head forward as if to place her chin on her chest. This action increases the diameter of the neck, making it more difficult for the enemy to grip and apply pressure against the windpipe. Since the attack is from the rear, the enemy has a distinct advantage at the outset, and the kunoichi must act swiftly and with great resolve to be effective.

With her right hand, as she steps to the left with her left foot to gain a wider stance and moves slightly outside the line of

FIGURE 99

FIGURE 100

FIGURE 101

FIGURE 102

FIGURE 103

engagement, the kunoichi executes a little-finger break on the enemy's right hand. At the same time, she swings her left arm in a wide arc (Figure 100), up and over her head to the left rear corner. This compresses the enemy's left hand against the jaw and the origin of the deltoid muscle. This pressure further breaks the enemy's grip.

Toeing out with the left foot and dropping the left arm down over the enemy's arms completely breaks his choke hold. Then, turn to the left rear and trap his arms between your driving left arm and the side of the body. The Dragon Lady then loads her right fist near her right ear in preparation for striking the enemy (Figure 101), who is now trapped by both of his elbows and is tilted forward to his right side. The next movement flows smoothly from this one in one continuous motion, taking advantage of the off-balance position of the enemy to take him to the mat.

Figure 102 shows the kunoichi stepping to the left rear with the left foot while pulling the enemy around by his arms and turning a full 270 degrees. Next, she strikes the enemy on the cheek or temple with the right hammer fist to stun him and drive him even further off balance. All of the enemy's weight is now on his right leg, and he cannot step forward to save himself with his left because the kunoichi can easily trip him with her left foot and throw him.

Stepping back with the left foot, the kunoichi moves out of the enemy's way and pulls him forward with her left hand. She continues to beat on the side of his head or drive her right forearm repeatedly against the enemy's left elbow and shoulder to further "break him down" to the mat. She finishes him off by applying the appropriate coupe de grâce (Figure 103).

Pulling the Enemy Over by His Own Hold

The concept of "reversing the situation" is basic to many of the techniques of ninjitsu. Female agents, like male agents, seldom strike the first blow, but true to the promise of many martial arts, when attacked, they kill in self-defense. In this movement, the enemy has managed to get a hold known in some circles as a waist cinch. His arms have encircled the kunoichi's waist but her arms are free. Obviously, the enemy is not going to depend on this hold for very long. The Dragon Lady could easily beat his brains out by striking backward with either elbow against his temple or the side of his neck until he changes the hold or is rendered senseless. So she must act quickly. Such a hold may be a stomach-pressing technique designed to "squeeze the air" out of the victim, but the kunoichi may not be able to pry his fingers off. The simplest trick is to use his own aggressive hold against him.

Figure 104 shows that the enemy has advanced and secured a rear bear hug hold from behind. The Dragon Lady, sensing this attack, has attempted to step forward and escape. As she did so, her arms naturally rose and so were not trapped by the attacker's encircling arms.

As the enemy cinches down with his hold (Figure 105), the Dragon Lady grabs both of his hands with her own to put a grip

FIGURE 104

FIGURE 105

FIGURE 106

FIGURE 107

on him, and the situation on a more equal footing. Simultaneously, she shoots her hip out to the enemy's weak side and turns perpendicular to his line of balance. (The *weak side* is a term which cannot be easily explained but which requires a great deal of experience. Basically, one develops a feel for the side on which the enemy places most of his weight and which way his inertia is going to carry him. Then you get under him so he falls over you.) By using the hold on the enemy's hands, the Dragon Lady pulls and lifts him over her back.

In Figure 106, the enemy is thrown to the ground on his back. The impact drives the wind out of his lungs and forces him to break his hold. If the enemy does not let go as he is being pulled over, she rides down with him. He will land on the bottom, and her weight will crush down on his shoulder. In this example, the enemy broke his fall with his left arm as he landed, and the Dragon Lady retained control of his right arm as he landed.

Before the enemy can recover from the fall or mount a successful counterattack, the Dragon Lady chops out with her right hand to the side of his neck to render him unconscious (Figure 107). To augment this strike, she pins his right arm to the ground with her right knee against his bicep.

5

ELBOW AND KNEE STRIKES

Many martial arts techniques are classified according to the range at which they are most effective. Techniques that are applied when the combatants are at extremely close range—body to body—are called grappling techniques. Such tactics were discussed in Chapter 2, "Escaping From Underneath." The taking-off-the-hand techniques in Chapter 3 are considered close range, since they involve releasing oneself from the enemy's grasp, but are not considered body to body.

The next series of strikes with the elbow and knee are referred to as intermediate, or mid-range, tactics. These tricks are designed to allow the Dragon Lady to free herself from the attacker's grip and disable him long enough for her to escape. (Long-range techniques, those executed at full extension of one's reach or those which require a step forward to initiate contact, are discussed in Chapter 6, "Combination Strikes.")

Elbow Strike

The Dragon Lady may also employ a slap-down block with both hands to close the distance to the adversary and bring him in range for the techniques you want to employ. From the basic stance, she strikes as the enemy advances toward her with arms

FIGURE 108

FIGURE 109

outstretched. Both wrists perform a downward chopping strike to forestall the intended hold (Figure 108). Likewise, if the enemy had grasped both of her wrists, she could attain this position by circling both hands inward to the centerline and breaking his hold.

The kunoichi then shifts her weight forward over the leading leg and extends her hands straight upward toward the enemy's head. Then her left hand may strike the enemy's cheek or rip his mouth with a thumb hook, or, as shown, grab the enemy by the ear and hair to control him (Figure 109). Simultaneously, she drives her right elbow, which she bends as she moves forward, into the side of the enemy's jaw just below the ear. The impact of this blow can easily knock out any opponent and may dislocate the jaw. This technique can also be used effectively as a close-range strike to the head and can be followed with another elbow strike to the temple or the side of the neck.

Forward Elbow Strike

Many techniques used by the Dragon Lady involve blocking with both arms together. This adds power to the deflection and, in most cases, is almost instinctive. The idea in practicing these movements is to follow the natural motion from its defensive application to a devastating counterattack. The rhythm for this is a one-two beat. In Figure 110, the Dragon Lady blocks by beating both arms against the enemy's advancing reach, knocking it down and to the outside.

The elbow, like the knee, is an excellent fighting tool. Figure 111 shows how the Dragon Lady immediately shifts forward, stepping in to close the gap between herself and the enemy, as well as to add her body weight to the strike. The kunoichi strikes out horizontally with her elbow at the level of the solar plexus, but since the enemy's head is brought forward by the deflection of his attack, the forearm strikes the forehead of the enemy. This jars the frontal lobes of the brain and drives the head back onto the neck to produce a whiplash injury.

FIGURE 110

FIGURE 111

Elbow Breaker

This is a crippling technique sometimes used by the kunoichi to stop an attacker before he has made bodily contact. Of course, in these situations the best defense is a good offense. Therefore, the Dragon Lady assumes a defensive stance that provides protection of the upper body by means of a high guard and in which the legs are positioned so that the lower body is balanced and centered over them (Figure 112). Furthermore, the kunoichi maintains a proper distance between herself and the enemy, making it necessary for him to advance and reveal his intent, thus giving her time to defend herself.

As the enemy's arm comes into range, the kunoichi whips out both forearms vertically along the line of engagement, trapping his arm between them and exerting crushing pressure on the elbow joint to strain or break it (Figure 113). This requires about twenty pounds of pressure. Note that leverage is increased when the wrist is held by one forearm and the other hand strikes just above the elbow, enhancing the effectiveness of the movement so that very little strength is needed to be disabling.

STRIKING WITH THE KNEE

There are several other targets besides the groin which might be easily attacked with the knee. In most instances, the knee lift is considered a close-range weapon, since it is ordinarily delivered when the enemy attempts to pin the agent's arms, making resistance difficult. The staggering effectiveness of the technique, however, encourages the clever kunoichi to investigate other uses.

Sometimes the enemy will reach forward in an attempt to obtain a hold on the shoulders or head of the agent. On those occasions, it may be necessary to check his attack by blocking with your arms. Circle both hands up and out and secure a firm grip on his biceps (Figure 114). This will induce him to grab your arms and try to resist your forward push against him. A subtle

FIGURE 112

FIGURE 113

FIGURE 114

trick of the kunoichi, derived from the ancient pressure point system of ninjitsu, is to press with the ball of the thumb against the nerves and blood vessels in the bend of the enemy's elbow. Alternatively, she might dig her sharpened and poisoned thumbnail into his arm.

If the enemy is clever, he will be aware that the Dragon Lady can strike him with her knee forcefully enough to disable him. He may hesitate in his advance or turn his leading knee in slightly to defend his groin. If that is the case, the Dragon Lady will merely take advantage of the opportunity, driving her knee into the inside of his thigh, midway between the hip and the knee (Figure 115). The object is to break the femur (the long bone of the leg).

This technique, like the previously discussed leg breaker, renders the enemy harmless. The minimum effect one could expect from such a blow is a severe muscle sprain and concurrent hematoma (bruising). If the strike is delivered from slightly

FIGURE 115

FIGURE 116

underneath the thigh, dislocation of the femur from the pelvis is possible. If the strike is directed almost horizontally against the thigh, dislocation of the knee below the point of impact is possible. Once this blow has been accomplished, the enemy's balance is severely broken and he can be easily thrown or eluded.

As a follow-up strike to the previous movement, the kunoichi pulls the enemy toward her, loads the knee strike again and drives upward diagonally against his ribs (Figure 116). The target is the "floating" rib (the one attached to the spine but not the sternum) on either side of the abdomen. If the strike is directed to the enemy's left side (as shown), the objective is to snap off the rib and drive it into the spleen. On the enemy's right, the target is the liver. *Either of these injuries is extremely serious.* Blood loss, internal bleeding, and shock are likely. Knocking the wind out of the enemy is the minimum effect. Observe that at this height, the blow could easily be directed against the solar plexus as well. A secondary target is the large diaphragm muscle just under the ribcage, since it lies more deeply in the abdominal cavity.

6

COMBINATION STRIKES

One of the ancient principles of temple boxing, handed down from *sensei* to adept, is the concept of attacking two places at one time. The idea is that one of the attacks will probably get through.

For the sake of balance, it is traditionally taught that if the left hand strikes, the right leg follow-strikes. Otherwise one would be guilty of what is known as double-weighting and be off balance.

PUTTING THE MOVES TOGETHER

In ninjitsu, most techniques follow one another in logical sequence to defeat the enemy. This is known as chain fighting, or stringing kicks and punches together to a successful conclusion.

The kunoichi takes a forward leaning stance with a low lead guard as the enemy advances (Figure 117). She seizes his wrist in her left hand and strikes the enemy's elbow upward from below with her right hand. This can easily break the elbow (Figure 118). She then drives a stomping side kick into the side of the enemy's knee. This breaks the joint, crippling him. She then maintains her hold on his broken arm to pull him into the strike (Figure 119).

FIGURE 117

FIGURE 118

FIGURE 119

FIGURE 120

FIGURE 121

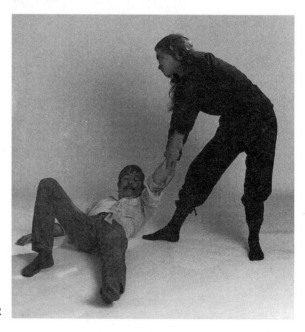

FIGURE 122

To follow up, the kunoichi drives a vicious side kick into the attacker's solar plexus to force the air out of his lungs and render him helpless (Figure 120). Maintaining her hold on the enemy's arm throughout, she swings her heel in a wide arc, outside the line of attack and up and back to strike the enemy's chin. At the same time, she pulls forward on his arm to further break his balance (Figure 121).

Pivoting on the heel of her left foot, the Dragon Lady completes the takedown or throw by dropping the enemy on his back to knock any remaining wind out of him and to set him up for the coup de grâce (Figure 122).

Palm Heel and Knee Lift

As shown in Figure 123, the heel of the hand is driven forcefully against the enemy's chin, throwing his head back and inducing a whiplash type of injury. Simultaneously, the opposite knee strikes upward into the enemy's groin with sufficient force to cripple him. Make both hits count.

As can be seen, the palm heel is a technique that can be used at extremely close range. Likewise, the knee lift can have devastating results.

Knee Lift and Elbow Strike

Figure 124 shows the logical progression from the previous strike. When the enemy bends forward after the first knee strike, the Dragon Lady again snaps her right leg upward to strike him in the chest. Her intention is to crush his sternum and damage the lungs. At the same time, the kunoichi drives the point of her left elbow straight down onto the enemy's spine. The idea is to dislocate one or more of the vertebrae or to chip and break off one or more of the bones of the spine and drop the enemy flat on his face.

FIGURE 123   FIGURE 124

Mirror Block (Outside) and Throat Strike

When an enemy reaches forward with his lead hand, the female ninja, knowing that it is easier to avoid the enemy's grasp than to escape from it, swings her left hand between herself and her enemy in a counterclockwise arc with the palm up. This move is similar to wiping fog from a mirror with a soft cloth, and thus is called the mirror block. She then strikes the edge of her opponents wrist with the edge of her hand (*shuto*), thus deflecting his arm across his centerline to interfere with any secondary attack he may intend with his other hand (Figure 125). Simultaneously, the Dragon Lady loads her right fist near her solar plexus in preparation for the counterstrike. This position can also be attained by escaping from the single wrist grab, in which the semicircular arc pulls one's hand free from the enemy's grasp.

FIGURE 125

FIGURE 126

To execute the counterattack, drop your fingers over the enemy's wrist, trapping his hand and deflecting his arm downward, out of the line of attack. The enemy can be pulled off balance by this hold if he is caught when he is not "set," or prepared to resist the tug. Without shifting forward, strike out strongly with a reverse sword-hand strike to the enemy's exposed throat (Figure 126). Maintain control of him by holding his wrist, and then take him down.

The throat strike is one of the most devastating techniques existing in the kunoichi arsenal. A moderate tap on the Adam's apple will produce breathlessness, and a solid hit can cause severe injury to the trachea and larynx, which may result in death.

Mirror Block (Inside) and Back Fist Strike

As the enemy reaches forward, execute an inside mirror block by whipping your lead hand up and outward in a clockwise arc to strike the inside of the enemy's wrist with the edge of your hand (Figure 127). The targets are the ulnar nerve on the little-finger side of the forearm and the radial nerve on the thumb side. The palm faces the enemy until the strike is made on the arm. A strike to these targets will temporarily numb the arm, thus breaking the momentum of the attack.

The kunoichi seeks not merely to deflect the attack of an enemy, but also to bring him in range for a counterstrike. To follow up, step forward and pull the enemy's arm down and to the side, then curl your fingers around his wrist. Even if this grip occurs higher on his arm, your hand will naturally slide down the decreasing diameter of his arm until the wrist is held firmly.

Strike out strongly with a back fist strike to the temple, aiming for the small bones just behind the eye (Figure 128). Hit with the back of the knuckles, rapping sharply as if knocking on a door. This hit will frequently break the skull bones, as they are relatively fragile at this point. A mild blow will stun the enemy;

FIGURE 127

FIGURE 128

FIGURE 129

FIGURE 130

a moderate hit will often render him unconscious; a strong one may cause concussion and death.

Hand Trap and Vertical Sword Hand

Many of the techniques of the Dragon Lady, and indeed the ninja, involve getting "behind" the enemy. Remembering that "a tiger cannot strike the one who rides his back," the Dragon Lady makes use of this principle, employing many subtle ploys to gain this advantageous position.

For example, if the kunoichi has executed a wrist grab release by circling her palm against the enemy's grip, and then reversed the action to grip his hand—or if she simply reaches out and takes hold of his arm—she has brought his elbow between them to prevent any further attack on his part (Figure 129). From this posture, the kunoichi can slip into any number of wristlock techniques, and also elect to finish off the enemy quickly.

Pull the enemy's arm down by means of the wristlock, i.e., by twisting his fingers or rotating his wrist so that the radius and ulna bones painfully grind against each other. Then, bend the enemy over forward to expose his upper back and neck. Strike down sharply on the back of his neck with the edge of your hand, shifting your weight forward to add force to the blow (Figure 130).

Aim for the base of the skull or the seventh cervical vertebra. Only a moderate blow will be effective, but jarring the bones of the neck to strike or pinch the spinal cord may stun the enemy. A heavy blow might dislocate the neck, causing whiplashlike injuries.

Hand Trap and Side Kick

When the leg is raised, as in performing a kick, the degree of balance is cut in half. Therefore, it is wise not only to prevent the enemy from attacking, but also to use him as a stabilizing force to maintain one's balance.

FIGURE 131

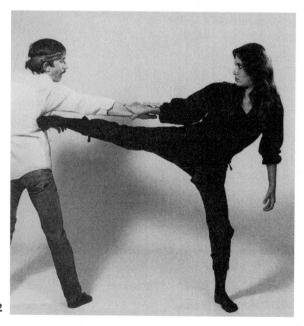

FIGURE 132

In this instance, use a sweeping mirror block to engage and deflect the arm of the enemy as it enters your sphere (Figure 131). Then catch hold of the enemy's wrist and pull him slightly toward you. He will probably resist the pull, lifting his trapped arm and turning to his side to brace with his leading leg. These actions expose the rib cage to a devastating attack from the chambered leading leg of the Dragon Lady (Figure 132).

Snap the kick outward from the waist, aiming just above the oblique muscles of the abdomen. Employ the more powerful muscles of the leg to drive the edge of your foot into the lower ribs of the enemy with the intention of breaking off the "floating," or lowest, rib and driving it into the enemy's lungs. Also, pulling him toward you adds to the impact of the hit.

7

THE STROKE OF DEATH

There were two types of secrets in the old ninjitsu: how to form the hand into a weapon and where to strike for maximum effect. Revealed here are five "death strokes" that may be used to kill, cripple, or maim virtually any attacker. They have been selected so that even the smallest and most frail user can overcome the mighty.

A large part of ninjitsu is attitude. One must be aware of danger, alert, and perceptive. Just as the kunoichi's stance reflects her intent to the enemy, his stance and bearing disclose his weak points and vulnerable areas to the well-trained eye.

Consider a scenario in which the Dragon Lady finds herself in a situation where a confrontation seems to be inevitable. Since we ninja value peace and harmony above all else, we have a preferred method of dealing with temples of violence: run away! If the enemy pursues, stare him down and show no fear, since fear is likely to only reinforce his aggressive behavior. Take note of where you are running; is he driving you into a blind alley, or are you leading him toward a public, well-lit area where help might be found?

If you are forced to fight, and this is only justified in cases of imminent peril to life or limb, then unleash the Dragon. Most

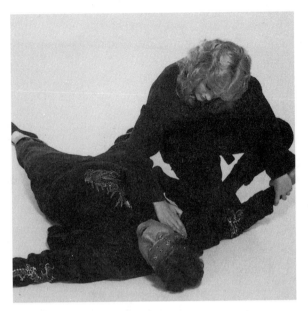

FIGURE 133

women fight only to escape; the kunoichi fights for life. She does not plan to survive an assault on her dignity and her person, and then hope for justice from others. She makes her own justice or dies trying.

In this section, certain vital and fatal points on the enemy's body are pinpointed and techniques for striking them so as to render him helpless are discussed. They are derived from the ancient art of *atemi-waza*, or striking movements (Figure 133), and are very useful for female agents.

"Mental toughness" is a phrase used by military men to mean self-discipline and calmness in the face of peril. It is insufficient to merely perform the actions of the ninja; one must grasp their principles and command the body. Few people consciously think about killing a fellow human being, yet there may be an occasion when such thoughts are necessary for survival—to know what must be done and do it. That is mental toughness. It need not be "proven" by placing oneself in danger and killing someone. It is expressed every day. Some people think that women are incapable of such psychological discipline, that they are too "emotional." But just remember the last time there was a death in the family, when you picked yourself up and went on because you knew that was all that could be done. *That* is mental toughness!

TO BLIND

"To deprive temporarily or permanently of the use of sight"

This is a severe tactic that will temporarily or permanently blind an assailant. Therefore, it must be reserved for only the most serious situations. It is the most simple and effective technique of self-defense you will ever learn—simple because it requires only one movement, and effective because it will painfully disorient any attacker.

This type of attack is accomplished at extremely close range using the fingers as the weapon. The target area includes the perimeter of the eye socket, which is designated by the bony structure of the orbit in the skull. Since the strike area is relatively soft, great harm can be done with only the fingertips.

There are numerous methods by which the finger jab can be delivered. We shall consider only two.

Stabbing With Fingers

This technique is used when you have only one hand free to attack. Stiffen all four fingers and round them slightly, then stab the extended fingers into the assailant's eyes. In some Chinese styles this technique is referred to as the finger fan and is recommended over the two-finger poke, which is normally taught because of the greater accuracy it provides. An analogy might be using a shotgun instead of a pistol.

The result of this attack upon the target is obvious. However, since this is the least likely of the three to succeed, we shall concern ourselves with the minimum damage it might inflict. A torn eyelid, usually the upper one, is the result of a sharp fingernail piercing the lid that has blinked at the last possible instant. Aside from the temporary blindness which this will cause, and the shock and trauma to the eye itself, there is also the likelihood of infection because of the small debris—dirt, germs, hair, or, in the case of the Dragon Lady, poison!—which will enter the eye along with the finger and the sharp nail. If the enemy survives the attack, this can be a more serious complication than the strike.

Twin Dragon Strike

The effect of the twin dragon strike (Figure 134) is far more devastating. The kunoichi executes a right upward fingertip strike to the eyes with the index and middle fingers of her right hand. The fingers are straight but not stiffened, as that might break them. The Dragon Lady drives the fingers into the eyes and follows through until the enemy is overcome. The result of this attack is the almost certain rupture of the eye bulb and the protrusion of the watery and gelatinous contents inside when the eye can no longer withstand the pressure against it, or when the fingernail penetrates and cuts the eyeball itself. Of course, this results in permanent blindness.

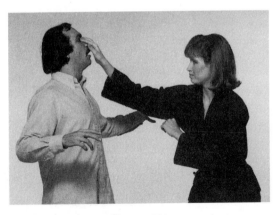

FIGURE 134

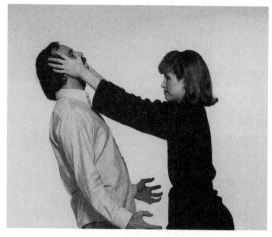

FIGURE 135

Thumb Gouge

The severity of an attack to the eyes should not be underestimated, and it should be recalled that courage and determination will often succeed where speed, strength, or even exotic technique have failed.

To execute the technique shown in Figure 135, grasp the enemy's head firmly with both hands. Your palms should be positioned against his ears. Simultaneously, with as much power as you can muster, gouge the thumbs into both of his eyes. This action will either rupture the eye, as in the preceding strike, or will force the eyeball from the socket by displacing it with the thumb. Again, this will result in permanent blindness.

Two points should be remembered when this type of attack is used. First, an attack to the eyes has a profound psychological effect on the enemy. A halfhearted effort will probably infuriate him; an effective attack will terrify him. To suddenly see nothing but blackness in the midst of pain is horrifying. Second, the pain itself is excruciating; to illustrate this you need only remember the last time you had an eyelash in your eye. Tremendous, shocking pain will prevail in both eyes, and uncontrollable watering always follows when a foreign object enters or touches the eye. Such watering naturally produces temporarily blurred vision even in the uninjured eye.

TO EMASCULATE

"To castrate, to deprive of strength and vigor, to make effeminate"

The second most vulnerable area of the male body is the groin. This includes the penis, testicles, scrotum, bladder, and central portion of the pubic bone. An attack to the groin will not kill and only rarely causes sterility. It is possible, however, to effectively cripple the enemy with this attack, thus rendering him useless for fighting. Bear in mind that an attack directly against the testicles has a built-in time delay. Pain from this strike takes almost one-and-a-half seconds to reach the brain and stun the enemy. Many ancient martial arts instructors schooled their disciples in executing a final "death spiral" type of movement to destroy their enemies if they were so attacked. Likewise, "grabbing the enemy by the balls" will take a second or so to be effective, so you could well be dead before he passes out from the pain. Therefore, the Dragon Lady directs her attack at the pubic arch of the pelvis, intending to enhance the effect of emasculation and render it more likely to succeed quickly.

Front Snap Kick

The front snap kick is the single most effective weapon to attack the groin. It allows you to keep a safe distance between you and the enemy and is therefore a long-range weapon. To perform this movement, lean slightly forward on your lead leg, bending it somewhat for balance. Bend the kicking leg by bringing the knee upward with the toes flexed (Figure 136).

Keep your hands up defensively and look the enemy directly in the eye, using your peripheral vision to spot the target. This is essential! The element of surprise is crucial in the execution of

FIGURE 136

this technique. *Never let the enemy suspect that you plan to attack his groin.* Many students are uncomfortable looking the enemy in the eye. Not so the Dragon Lady, who defies the enemy to strike, thus luring him in. However, if that is not advisable, fix your attention on his chest and do not look at the target until the kicking foot has left the ground. Furthermore, it is natural to gather momentum for this kick by "winding up," or swinging the leg behind the body. This error is known as "telegraphing" and can be defeated by lifting the knee rather than winding up. This also contributes to the snapping action of the kick, making it quicker and less likely to be blocked or deflected (Figure 137).

Snap the foot forward and upward, striking the target with the ball of the foot. Kick "through" the target, not merely at it, and snap the leg back as quickly as you shot it out to prevent the enemy from catching it and blocking the kick or reversing the situation. Aim for the pubic arch, the point on the front of the pelvis directly above the penis.

FIGURE 137

The results of the snap kick to the groin are as follows: rupture of the bladder from the percussion of a solid kick or from a fracture of the pubic bone, with consequent blood and urine in the abdominal cavity. The symptom of this is severe tenderness, pain, and rigidity in the lower quadrant. These are the *minimum* effects one can expect from a squarely placed blow. Even a poorly placed strike will often intimidate the enemy or render him harmless. The center of the public bone is the weakest and most probable point of fracture. The inability to walk due to the pinching and abrading pain of the pubic bones rubbing together will induce severe nausea, all of which will contribute to bringing the enemy to a prone position.

In order for the kick to penetrate to the underside of the frontal pubic bone, it must drive through the penis and the scrotum. As these tissues are comparatively soft, this is not a difficult feat. From even a minimally effective kick, disruption of the urethra, bleeding and urine in the scrotal sack, and tremendous pain will result. Some schools teach that the strike is done with the instep, but these bones are small, and while they may temporarily disable the enemy, the crippling effect of the described strike is only possible with the ball of the foot.

Naturally, any injury to the groin involves the possibility of infection and peritonitis. The testicles are very mobile within the scrotum. Pain, shock, loss of breath, nausea, vomiting, unconsciousness, and sometimes death (as a delayed effect) follow such a strike. The possibility of sterility from a crushed testicle or impotence resulting from injury to the penis clearly establishes this as the most effective technique for emasculating the enemy.

TO DEAFEN

"To make deaf, to stun with noise, to deprive of the sense of hearing"

This technique provides a simple and effective method of rendering the enemy unconscious and most likely permanently deafening him. The secret lies in the fact that by cupping the palms, a small column of air may be pressurized into the auditory canal to rupture the eardrum. This was once known as boxing the ears. As a straw may be driven into a tree by the wind of a tornado, so the sudden increase in pressure within the ear acts to drive the tympanic membrane out of place. Due to the extremely sensitive nature of the nerves in this area, especially those concerned with balance, this strike can easily produce a concussion and kill the enemy.

Suppose the enemy advances with the intent of seizing the kunoichi by the shoulders or head (Figure 138). Although he is menacing, she fixes her gaze intently and shifts slightly forward to meet him as he comes on. When acting in self defense, it might be more advisable to fall back and lure in the enemy. Even if he grabs you around the head, you can still strike and do him in. The important thing to remember is to keep both hands low, as shown.

FIGURE 138

Double Ear Slap

Swing both arms down and out, and then upward in wide semicircular arcs to slap the enemy soundly and simultaneously on both ears. The practice method for this is to simply swing your arms out as far as you can in front of yourself and clap your palms together. From this it will be easily observed that sufficient force can be generated to overcome the enemy. The effects of this strike are profound. First, since the head is not allowed to "roll with the blow," the impact is doubled. This may cause a concussion, in which the enemy is immediately rendered unconscious, and the possibility of death. Secondly, rupture of the eardrum is probable, along with the disruption of the inner ear and loss of balance. When this is the case, many of the small blood vessels in the auditory canal, eustachian tube, and inner ear also burst. The evidence of this is bleeding, either profuse or subtle, from the ear itself. Third, from the configuration of the

FIGURE 139

FIGURE 140

cupped palms, the heel or edge of the hands may make contact with the rear of the enemy's zygomatic arch (cheekbone). Should this occur, it is likely that the facial vein will be broken, resulting in a large bruise on the side of the face, and that the facial nerve will be damaged, causing numbness (Figures 139 and 140).

So it can be clearly seen that even a small fighter, acting with resolve and determination, can knock out a much larger and stronger opponent.

TO CRIPPLE

"To deprive of the use of a limb, especially a leg"

While most of the tricks in this section are directed toward the more vulnerable targets of the body, the kunoichi are also skilled in effectively crippling the enemy in other ways. For the weak at heart who find debilitating the enemy repugnant, the following may be of some service. But these, of course, cannot be employed until the enemy has been brought under some degree of control.

Leg Breaker

The most obvious reason for employing this technique is to insure that the enemy will not be able to pursue and reengage you in combat. Make sure that the enemy is down and at least partially stunned. Lift the enemy's leg by the ankle and hold it against your thigh (Figure 141). Do not interlock the fingers; you must be able to let go if the enemy counterattacks. Stomp down on the enemy's knee with the heel of the opposite foot to dislocate the joint and tear the tendons behind the leg. When the kneecap is driven down, the joint is hyperextended, the muscles are crushed and torn, the tendons are stretched and ripped free of their anchoring attachments to the bones, the tibial artery and vein may be ruptured, and the tibial nerve is certainly traumatized. Nausea and unconsciousness may result from the intense pain.

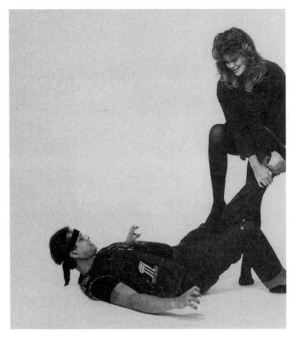

FIGURE 141

Furthermore, if surgical repair is not soon forthcoming, the enemy will be permanently crippled. It takes approximately forty pounds of pressure to break the leg in this manner. A severe sprain is the minimal injury one could expect from this movement.

Back Breaker

Another technique that insures the enemy will not follow you is the back breaker. It is less an attack on the spine than a double knee-drop strike to the abdomen. Once the enemy has been taken down, seize his hair and pull his head back to set him up for the strike (Figure 142). Drop directly onto his back with both knees, letting your full weight drive him against the floor. The hair pull prevents him from slipping away and bends his back so that the percussive impact of the knees hyperextends the thoracic vertebrae. This may cause a fracture or a rupture of the

FIGURE 142

intervertebral discs. Any such injury always produces the possibility of damage to the spinal cord. Should that occur, the enemy will be temporarily paralyzed (if the cord is only "bruised") or permanently paralyzed below the point of the injury. If the knees land off the spine, the weight can crush the ribs and underlying lungs, liver, spleen, or kidneys. Finally, because the head is pulled back when the blow lands, it is probable that the enemy will incur whiplash as well. The minimum effect is to knock the wind out of him.

TO KILL

"To deprive of life, to slay, to render dead"

We said at the outset that the use of these techniques of death and destruction is not to be taken lightly. The Dragon Lady earns her reputation as a vicious and ruthless fighter with these tools, and others may easily apply them in self-defense. In that regard, remember that we are speaking of the defense of the self. This encompasses far more than the physical aspects, and must include the psychological considerations of assault or rape. The Dragon Lady of old was aware of these dangers and risked them anyway. For whatever reasons, such as patriotism, revenge, or duty, she was and is today among the finest fighters ever trained.

Today, the need to kill a fellow human being can seldom be justified. Yet that need may arise, in defense of one's own life, honor, virtue, or in defense of another who is helpless. The taking of a life does no one honor, but if it must be done, do it quickly and efficiently. Rely on yourself alone, because help is seldom at hand, and justice, even if you live, is rare.

Palm Heel

For this strike the target is the point of the chin, and the striking surface is the heel of the hand. On the chin, the nerves which control the action of the tongue meet those which serve the face. Damage to this point will result in numbness of the face itself, and in some cases loss of control of the tongue. The enemy may well suffocate as a result of swallowing his own tongue.

Place the forearm directly against the enemy's chest on his centerline with your fingers pulled back to expose the palm heel fist. Drive the heel of the hand straight upward to strike the chin forcefully from below (Figure 143). The primary effect of this attack results from the whiplash injury as the head is driven back. Sliding up the chest makes the punch almost impossible to block and has an effect very similar to the uppercut in boxing. This strike lifts the enemy's chin and exposes his throat for the coup de grâce, or death blow, though it may kill the enemy by itself due to the concussion.

Sword Hand

An attack to the throat is considered a medium-range tactic. Striking the neck from the front, side, or back can render most attackers unconscious. Here we shall deal with only one method of attacking: a blow to the trachea (Adam's apple) with the edge of the hand, which can easily kill an enemy. The target area lies

FIGURE 143

from the underside of the chin to the jugular notch between the clavicles. The weapon employed to attack this area is known in martial arts circles as the sword-hand fist, and extends along the outer edge of the hand between the base of the little finger and the hamate bone just above the wrist.

To deliver the attack, form the sword hand by flexing the edge of the hand to create the proper tension. Extend the fingers with the knuckles together and cock the thumb inward to tighten the muscle on the little finger side of the hand. Load the fist near the opposite ear, cross the chest, and strike out strongly, chopping at the target. Remember to follow through for maximum effect (Figure 144).

The results of this attack are profound. Rupture of the trachea would result in a quick death due to massive blood loss, or such an attack may result in a delayed death due to blood clots in the brain. Second, injury may cause spasms of the heart and lungs,

FIGURE 144

ultimately resulting in shortness of breath, irregular heartbeat, and death. Third, if the phrenic nerve (which controls the diaphragm) is injured, the enemy may be unable to catch his breath, a condition which will continue until normal functioning can be restored or death occurs from oxygen starvation.

Finally, death may occur as a result of the direct percussive damage to the trachea. Swelling or severe bleeding in the throat and partial or total blockage of the windpipe by the epiglottis or ruptured tissue will soon choke the enemy. In any event, the effect of this double-action strike insures a quick and relatively painless death.

The effectiveness of this blow may be demonstrated on oneself by striking the Adam's apple with only *one-twentieth* of the power required to injure someone. *A slight tap is quite sufficient!*

8

THE MEDITATION

Now that you have read the deadly secrets of the Dragon Lady, return to the beginning and read through twice more. In this way, the information will be placed in the subconscious of your mind, ready to be recalled and used if needed. If you are more adventurous, study and practice the techniques as well, but do so with great care and patience. Mastery does not come quickly, but rather one step at a time.

When I first began in ninjitsu, I did so with some resentment because I was expected to study. Then I began to appreciate the superior physical and mental conditioning that was the benefit of such an art. Later still, the philosophy of the oneness with Nature was revealed to me, and I understood the Way of Knowledge, the Silent Way. Now I practice for health and the companionship of my few students, for the study of a single system may consume a lifetime.

To withdraw from the world to practice the Dark Art, you learned *sanchin* (sitting zen) meditation preparatory to learning the exotic techniques of the kunoichi. Now, to return to the "real world," you must learn the most basic of *kuji-kiri* ("nine cuts") relaxation exercises. They are used to calm the mind and restore balance to the spirit.

FIGURE 145

Sit in the Lotus position with the back straight, as in figure 145, palms on knees, eyes closed. Relax. Inhale, deeply filling the lungs completely from bottom to top. Exhale and picture three lines, one above the other (Japanese kanji for *san*, or three), three times. Inhale again, and exhale as before, visualizing the number *ni* (two horizontal lines, one above the other, representing "two" in Japanese) three times. Repeat once more, this time imagining the kanji *i* , or one, three times on the exhalation (*i* is shown as a single horizontal line).

You are now in a relaxed state of mind. You feel good to be relaxed; you feel better than before. You have gained confidence through your study and practice. Now you are ready to walk like a dragon, without fear, capable and ready, confident and proud, a ninja Dragon Lady.

Postscript

After all of this discussion, it may seem that a woman's self-defense is an intricate and complicated series of techniques that require years of practice and study. Not so. Any one of these methods can be used to ward off an attacker; any two will enable you to defend yourself adequately against most aggressors; and any three will make you formidable in combat.

It is not necessary to become a martial arts master to protect yourself. Even if you have done no more than read this book, you already have enough information to inflict serious injury. If you learn only one thing from this text it should be simple and effective for you. One lesson often taught to female agents of the ninja is the "high balls and low balls" rule. The eyes and the testicles are the two most vulnerable targets on the male attacker. If you cannot get to one, for example, poke him in the eyes, then attack the other, for instance, with a groin pull. It is almost certain that one of these targets will present itself during the battle. If not, wait until the opportunity appears.

If you learn nothing else from your study of these methods, remember the three rules of self-defense: "Never take a hit you can avoid. Never strike until there is an opening in the enemy's defense. And, when the opportunity does appear, strike hard, strike fast, show no mercy."

This is the Way of the Dragon Lady. May it serve you well.